GREAT IRISH SPEECHES

RICHARD ALDOUS

Quercus

Contents

Foreword

By Colm Tóibín

In January 2007, a few weeks before his death, I spoke to Arthur Schlesinger in New York about John F. Kennedy's visit to Ireland in June 1963. When I explained the impact that Kennedy's glamour and eloquence had had on Ireland, Schlesinger told me that many of Kennedy's speeches in Ireland had been carefully crafted and some of them had contained a message for the Irish government. For example, according to Schlesinger, a number of Kennedy's advisers, including Schlesinger himself, took a dim view of the censorship of books in Ireland, which had continued into the 1960s, and believed that the official Irish view that James Joyce was 'a dirty writer' needed to change. Thus they made sure that John F. Kennedy's speech to the Joint Houses of the Oireachtas in Ireland contained a reference to James Joyce, which might have seemed casual to the assembled audience, but was placed in the speech deliberately as a way of suggesting that those in power in Ireland might wake up to Joyce's importance and value.

If the history of England between, say, 1782 and now has been a history of gradual change, the slow creation of consensus, the building of democratic values and tolerance through quiet reform, two steps forward, one step back, then the history of Ireland has been more difficult to read, reform often happening in the shadow of revolt, gradual change in the wake of cataclysm, consensus often coming hand in glove with intolerance and sectarianism. Over these two centuries language in Ireland has often seemed an aspect of performance, eloquence itself has at times seemed more influential than laws; poems and plays and speeches have often been more powerful than actions. Thus a history of *Great Irish Speeches* can be as close to a history of Ireland as a history of Irish reform or Irish rebellion.

In some speeches, such as John F. Kennedy's to the Joint Houses of the Oireachtas in 1963, it is necessary to read the words forensically, searching for clues, hidden meanings and ambiguities. Both Daniel O'Connell and Charles Stewart Parnell, for example, as orators, understood that they were speaking to their own people and to the British government at the same time. They were suggesting that they, as constitutional nationalists, believers in Parliament and upholders of the law, stood between the law and those who might break the law. Their power arose from the great ambiguity of their position, which they expressed with immense subtlety in their public speeches.

O'Connell, therefore, could speak in Mullaghmast in County Kildare in 1843 about 'the same resolution not to violate the peace; not to be guilty of the slightest outrage', and soon afterwards, in the same speech, he could say that 'we came here to express our determination to die to a man, if necessary, in the cause of old Ireland.' His listeners, too, came in a number of guises: those who actually believed what he said – the mixture of the dreamy and the pragmatic – and those who understood that his positioning of himself through his eloquence at the very centre of debate gave him a sort of power, which could easily be removed from him by the English if he overstepped the mark laid down for him, or by his compatriots should he seem too timid.

There must have been, among his listeners, many who thought that he was talking rubbish but understood that he had harnessed a powerful national movement, which could further be harnessed by more radical and revolutionary forces. I know this not only because of books I have read, but because he spoke outside Enniscorthy in the same period as he spoke at Mullaghmast. I was born in that town in 1955. Men who saw him speak knew that his references to rich harvests and sweet meadows and greenest fields were pure nonsense in a country where the system of land-holding was a major source of vicious poverty and would lead, within two years, with the help of a potato blight, to serious famine.

Men saw him speak in Enniscorthy who later became Fenians, just as some were already members of the Young Ireland movement. They saw O'Connell as a catalyst for change and not as an enemy. But their words, when they got a chance to speak, would be more fiery, less compromising. My grandfather and his brother were sworn into the Fenians by men who had seen O'Connell speak outside Enniscorthy. When my father showed me the field where O'Connell spoke, he knew about this because he had heard it from his own father.

By the time Parnell rose to power, there were people in Ireland who saw his eloquence in London, and indeed the Land League in Ireland led by Michael Davitt, as just two parts of a movement which would lead to an Irish republic. When Parnell said in Cork in 1885: 'Nobody could point to any single action of ours in the House of Commons or out of it which was not based upon the knowledge that behind us existed a strong and brave people' and when he used the word 'invincible' to describe his movement, it would have been clear to his listeners that he was not merely talking about his power as a parliamentarian but invoking the whiff of sulphur, the shadow of Captain Moonlight, which were parts of his aura.

Throughout the 19th century, in the wake of the failed rebellions of the past, Irish orators invoked history, making its neat completion a sort of destiny. The story of Ireland became not only the story of oppression but the story of a struggle for liberty which could end only in golden success. The rhetoric surrounding this offered James Joyce, for one, some wonderful comic moments in *Ulysses*, especially when he wrote about the execution of Robert Emmet. Nationalism, for Joyce, was a joke from which he was trying to recover. But Joyce did not find the fall of Parnell funny. Parnell stood alone for him in his nobility, his pure dignity and the tragedy of his defeat.

My grandfather and his associates paid no attention to the priests and the bishops who denounced the Fenians in sermons such as that by Bishop Moriarty of Kerry in 1867. There were always priests who would hear confessions and give the sacraments to members of revolutionary organizations who were sworn to secrecy in the cause of Ireland. The poet W.B. Yeats saw the fall of Parnell as a great opportunity for culture to replace politics in Ireland, but Yeats missed what was really happening, that a new sort of politics came to replace Parnell. Men like my grandfather were moving into positions of power and influence in the Gaelic Athletic Association and the Gaelic League, ostensibly non-political organizations, associated with sport and Irish culture. From there, they were building a revolutionary movement.

But the defeat of Parnell by the Catholic clergy and also the series of land acts passed in Westminster which created land-owners out of a potentially revolutionary landless class slowly built the bedrock of a new society in Ireland, which would become, despite the diehards in its midst, a very conservative country. Although James Larkin became a hero, and has a statue in O'Connell Street between the monuments to O'Connell and Parnell, he and his movement lost first at the hands of the employers and then at the hands of the nationalists who believed that the Labour movement would have to wait.

I remember in the late 1980s and early 1990s having occasion, as a journalist, to sit at meetings in the boardroom of Independent Newspapers, once owned by William Martin Murphy, the arch-enemy of both Larkin and W.B. Yeats, and discovering, to my surprise, that a portrait of Murphy hung in pride of place in the headquarters of what was still, and is still, the largest newspaper group in Ireland. James Larkin, the great speechmaker, had a statue in the main thoroughfare of the city; Murphy, who never said a memorable word, was the one whose legacy remained most quietly intact. Oratory in Ireland has often been a way for the weak to make their mark; real and abiding victory often belonged to those who remained quiet.

What we must look for in these speeches besides eloquence and ambiguity and elements of double-speak is what is left out. Just as O'Connell made no reference to systems of land-ownership, no nationalist, speaking for the Irish people, made any reference to the fact that the majority of people in the northeastern corner did not wish to be part of Ireland's destiny. Speeches from the north, when they came, had no ambiguity; they used the same language as the diehards in the south of the country, explaining that they would not compromise.

Yet there were moments in this story when someone reading the newspapers and listening to speeches could have been easily fooled. 1914 was one of those moments. John Redmond seemed to be in full control of the Volunteers, and if he could lead them to help gallant little Belgium in the company of their northern compatriots, then a coming together of the two traditions in Ireland must have seemed possible. And the split in the Volunteers must have seemed a minor affair. But men like my grandfather and grand–uncle, part of the 13,000 who became the minority Irish Volunteers, remained Fenians. They were deeply determined to organize an armed rebellion against the British, as much because of the opposition of northern Protestants than despite such opposition. Slowly, in these years, they watched as figures from cultural nationalism, such as Patrick Pearse, through a number of key speeches, such as the one given over the grave of O'Donovan Rossa in 1915, which invoked the dead, began to radicalize themselves and those around them.

This business of Ireland as the place where the dead had more power than the living, where funeral orations could inflame public opinion, made compromise difficult. My grandfather and his friends took part in the 1916 Rebellion and were interned in English jails afterwards, where they re-grouped and prepared for a final revolution which would, they hoped, remove the British from Ireland in the name of what Pearse called 'the dead generations'. They did not discuss social policy in those English prison camps, they were not reading Marx or Connolly; they remained romantic nationalists, deeply suspicious of anyone who would treat with the enemy. They saw Michael Collins, once he had signed the Treaty, in the same way as they had seen O'Connell, Parnell and Redmond, as a figure useful only up to a certain point, as a front, as a smokescreen, someone easily discarded. Collins, in making his argument for the Treaty he had signed with the British to the Dáil in 1921, understood he was speaking to ghosts as much as to living beings: 'Deputies have spoken about whether dead men would approve of it, and they have spoken of whether children yet unborn will approve of it, but few of them have spoken as to whether the living approve of it. In my own small way I tried to have before my mind what the whole lot of them would think of it.' James Joyce's the living and the dead had come together as a force to be reckoned with. They were ready to fight a civil war.

As much as you watch for eloquence in these years, you watch for silence. The silence of employers like William Martin Murphy, whose power would not be weakened by independence or partition; the silence of the Catholic bishops who knew that partition and the new state would offer them almost unlimited power.

Thus the battles which now took place in the new state were not about the creation of a just society but were between intellectuals who sought freedom of speech or freedom for minorities. Once more, in his eloquent speech to Seanad

Éireann in 1925, W.B. Yeats would invoke the dead in his efforts to have the rights of the living recognized: 'We are one of the great stocks of Europe. We are the people of Burke; we are the people of Grattan; we are the people of Swift, the people of Emmet, the people of Parnell. We have created the most of the modern literature of this country.' A quarter of a century later, it is notable that Noël Browne's effort to improve the lives of the living, his rhetoric free of any mention of the destiny of the nation or the power of the dead, did not work.

My uncle fought on de Valera's side in the civil war and was interned by the Free State, as his father had been by the British. He was a founder-member of the Fianna Fáil party and my father became a member as soon as he was old enough. About the other side, Cumann na nGael, then the Blueshirts and then Fine Gael, my father used to say that you could salute them if you met them on the street, but if you ever voted for them, your right hand would wither off. In Enniscorthy, as I was growing up, party politics was not about policy; it was tribal.

Ireland north and south vied with one another as to which could be the more sectarian state. This was most eloquently put by James Craig in 1933: 'They still boast of Southern Ireland being a Catholic state. All I boast of is that we are a Protestant Parliament and a Protestant state.'

A few times in these two centuries of speechmaking a new rhetoric appears. It is often direct and free of poetry. It means business and lacks eloquence. Seán Lemass's speech at Clery's ballroom in 1955 is one such speech – it is pragmatic and serious. It was not designed to stir up feeling but to cause a change in policy and was followed by legislation. It created the country into which I was born, where the ruling party, Fianna Fáil, would from now on use the rhetoric of dreams only when it suited them, but would be just as happy talking about job creation, taxation and social policy.

The rest of these speeches read like snapshots of the country I grew up in. My father took me to Wexford in June 1963 to see John F. Kennedy honouring the statue of John Barry. In 1969, as a highly politicized youth who had worked for Fianna Fáil in the campaign, I took a lift to the counting of votes in Wexford town from a Labour party candidate who believed, with Brendan Corish, our local TD, that the seventies would be socialist.

I saw Terence O'Neill make his crossroads speech on television. I remember the extraordinary and passionate eloquence of Bernadette Devlin. I watched Jack Lynch say that the Irish government could no longer stand by. I remember the election of Liam Cosgrave as taoiseach in 1973 and, with friends, did imitations of his clipped and uncharismatic rhetorical style. I saw Charles Haughey make his 'living away beyond our means' speech on television in 1980. I felt I understood what was happening in those years; I was alert to the Republic of Ireland as a place which had its own social and economic difficulties, a society which sought only stability in the north but found it difficult to say out loud that it no longer cared about a united Ireland.

In retrospect, John Hume, through his speeches and interviews, emerges as a towering and visionary figure. His speech in Newcastle, County Down, in 1981 set out the blueprint for an agreed Ireland to be shaped for the sake of the living rather than the dead. He used an old rhetoric, full of eloquent phrases and the languages of ideals and aspirations, but he was saying something new and courageous. He was, with Seán Lemass, an Irish political leader who could insist that he meant what he was saying literally. He did not speak in hints and nudges, but sought to set out an actual blueprint which would have far-reaching results in his speeches.

Over the past 30 years, Irish politicians have moved between the language of plain talk and the language of high idealism. Des O'Malley, beginning in his Dáil speech in 1985, attempted to remove all flourishes from his public discourse, to use plain sentences and a modest tone. Alan Dukes, as leader of Fine Gael, was to use a similar style, as did politicians such as Mary Harney and Mícheál Martin. Garret FitzGerald, who became taoiseach first in 1981, managed to present himself as a saviour of his people from bad economic policies and narrow social vision, as a politician who would lead his people towards rational reform and inclusive politics. He spoke with idealism and openness of his great intentions, many of which came to fruition only later when he was out of power.

Just as the rhetoric of Éamon de Valera took its bearings from the early poetry of Yeats, so too Mary Robinson as President of Ireland used a language of poetic inclusion, in which words could be wielded to suggest a great deal, a style which took its bearings from the poetry and prose writings of poets Eavan Boland and Séamus Heaney. In her speeches, she moved the periphery to the centre and suggested that the centre would be healthier and happier after such a move. She also used silence, the art of seeming to listen and consider, in the same way as the bishops had done, making her public statements seem all the more powerful for that.

The government had a veto on her speeches, but not on her silences. Thus she could, early in her presidency, invite gay men and lesbians to Áras an Uachtaráin and merely welcome them, include them. She developed a passionate rhetoric of human rights and high-minded social ethics which was new in Irish public life. I attended Albert Reynolds's first press conference as taoiseach early in Robinson's presidency and watched him saying that changing the laws against homosexuality would not be a priority for his government. This makes the action of Máire Geoghegan-Quinn, a Fianna Fáil politician from the west of Ireland, Minister for Justice in his government, all the more brave and astonishing in changing the law. Her speech to an almost empty Dáil in 1993 on the matter reads like a new sort of utterance in Ireland, high idealism which was to be matched by swift action in the form of legislation. She spoke of ideals from a position of power. So much Irish eloquence before her had arisen from powerlessness.

Slowly, then, politicians north and south, began to use the rhetoric of reaching out to the other side, or to the churches, or to minority communities, or to the dead, almost as though it came naturally to them. Sudden conversion became as popular as sport, and the rhetoric of half-baked conviction served up as sincerity, bravery and leadership became the price we had to pay for peace on the island. There were notable exceptions to this, including the socialist Joe Higgins, the most eloquent and angry parliamentarian of his generation, whose speech to the Dáil in 2002 about 'Ansbacher man' is merely one example of his great contribution to Irish speechmaking.

Bertie Ahern's speech in Westminster in 2007 comes, after two centuries of eloquence, as a culminating event. The work of revisionist historians who had tried to suggest that the story of Ireland is more complex than the simple story of conquest, revolt from tyranny and then freedom, who had tried to suggest that the relationship between Ireland and Britain had many strands, was given voice by the taoiseach: 'British settlement, organized and otherwise, has given the island of Ireland a British tradition too – not just in history and language, borders and politics, but in a thriving community of unionist people proud of who they are, where they come from, and what they hope for. They are a living bridge between us.'

It was interesting to hear the living invoked in the speech which also remembered the dead. Ahern ended by quoting from the speech which John F. Kennedy had made to the Dáil in 1963 when he said that Ireland's hour had come, when he referred to Ireland as 'an isle of destiny'. Kennedy's speechwriters would have been proud – words made in Washington for utterance in Ireland now being repeated in the Mother of Parliaments where O'Connell and Parnell, as speechmakers, had established their power. And James Joyce might have looked on too, from the special gallery reserved for him in all places where words come first, letting loose perhaps at least two cheers in the name of both the living and the dead, or shaking his head to suggest an even greater eloquence which lies between words, or in the gaps between rhetoric and real meaning, which many of these speeches display with superb and beguiling artistry.

Introduction

Ours is an age obsessed with secrecy. Freedom of information, the annual media excitement surrounding documents released under the 30-year rule from national archives, and vast tribunals of enquiry: all offer the hope that we might uncover 'the real truth' hidden from us by those in power. Conversely what is said or written publicly is often regarded as, at best, misleading ('spin') or, at worst, outright lies. Mechanisms that encourage transparency offer the chance to see a more complete picture. Yet they also offer a false trail. For in our demand to see what is hidden, we often ignore a more obvious truth: it is in the arena of public discourse that the battle of ideas takes place. That contest shapes the minds and passions of successive generations. The Victorian writer, Mark Pattison, called this process 'the active warfare of opinion'. In that conflict, few weapons are as effective as rhetoric.

Nowhere is this observation more applicable than in the story of modern Ireland. It may be a cliché to claim that the Irish have a way with words, but the skill deployed in the pages of this book shows how commanding an instrument they can be. The power of language and the effect it might have on an audience have been indelibly bound together in the course of Irish history. In his book *Inventing Ireland* Declan Kiberd demonstrated how, at critical moments, Irish leaders thought of themselves in dramatic, even theatrical, terms. Political platforms, the floor of a parliamentary chamber, courtroom docks, radio and TV studios and the steps of public buildings served many purposes, but they all offered, among other things, a stage upon which actors might play the part they had chosen (or history had chosen for them).

Selecting 50 from so many exceptional speeches on offer was not an easy task. This collection is one of Irish men and women speaking about Ireland. It might just have easily been entitled 'The speeches that changed Ireland'. This means that some great Irish orators have been omitted, not least Edmund Burke, because Ireland did not provide the primary focus of their work or thought. On the other side, an exception has been made for the speech by US president John F. Kennedy, a representative of the Irish diaspora.

The book starts in the 18th century with Henry Grattan. He heralded an era of rhetoric that was not only recorded but secular; the 17th century, by contrast, had spoken mainly in sermons. Only two men are given more than one speech: Éamon de Valera, the dominant figure of 20th-century Irish history; and Bertie Ahern, who in one speech provides the last (or at least the most recent) word on the Irish Question, and in another raises some of the uncertainties of identity that contemporary Ireland faces in the 21st century.

The speeches divide in the broadest sense into those of the head and those of the heart. Many display remarkable powers of analysis, setting out rigorous arguments to influence opinion by sheer force of intellect. Others gain their authority from the passion and context of their delivery, as a speaker finds an oratorical elixir to inspire or capture a public mood. Only occasionally do both occur at the same time. When they do, such as in de Valera's response to Churchill, the result transcends its own time and speaks to ours.

It is public expression of thought that provides men of action with moral authority. Language, wrote W.B. Yeats, 'becomes persuasive, immortal even, if held to amid the sway of events'.

Richard Aldous   *Monkstown, County Dublin, 2007*

'Spirit of Swift! Spirit of Molyneux!'

Henry Grattan
(1746–1820)

Speech to the Irish House of Commons, Dublin, 16 April 1782

HENRY GRATTAN
'Spirit of Swift! Spirit of Molyneux!'

13

Henry Grattan was just one of Ireland's many great orators, but he was unique in having a Parliament named after him. From the late 17th century onwards, resentment about Ireland's limited control over its own trade and legislative affairs had fostered a sense of Irish identity among some Protestants who in all other respects identified with Britain. Known as the Patriots, they set their sights on the prize of legislative independence for the Parliament in Dublin. Early supporters included the political philosopher, William Molyneux, and the dean of St Patrick's Cathedral in Dublin, Jonathan Swift. They were revered by later generations of Patriots, the most famous of whom was Henry Grattan, the Member of Parliament for Charlemont.

In 1779–80 Grattan led a campaign for free trade, and afterwards pressed for a 'declaration of the rights of Ireland'. This campaign was ultimately successful, even if the relative legislative freedom it brought was shortlived. Rebellion in 1798 prompted London to abolish 'Grattan's Parliament' (which voted itself out of existence) and create a United Kingdom of Great Britain and Ireland.

Grattan lived to see this and to refine his historical legacy accordingly. The speech below is perhaps his best known. Some of its most famous lines, including 'Spirit of Swift! Spirit of Molyneux! Your genius has prevailed', were probably added by Grattan in old age, thus disproving the old adage that you cannot rewrite history.

BIOGRAPHY

Henry Grattan was born in Dublin in 1746 and educated at Trinity College. Elected to the Dublin Parliament in 1775 as the Member for Charlemont, he became one of the foremost Patriot MPs in the Irish Parliament. He retired from politics after the passing of the Act of Union, but was lured back to the fray in 1805 to sit as an MP at Westminster. He then devoted his energy to Catholic emancipation, a cause he never lived to see fulfilled. Grattan died in London in 1820 and was buried at Westminster Abbey. His sons James and Henry followed in the family tradition by sitting in the House of Commons.

I am now to address a free people: ages have passed away, and this is the first moment in which you could be distinguished by that appellation.

I have spoken on the subject of your liberty so often, that I have nothing to add, and have only to admire by what heaven-directed steps you have proceeded until the whole faculty of the nation is braced up to the act of her own deliverance.

I found Ireland on her knees, I watched over her with a paternal solicitude; I have traced her progress from injuries to arms, and from arms to liberty. Spirit of Swift! Spirit of Molyneux! Your genius has prevailed. Ireland is now a nation. In that new character I hail her, and bowing to her august presence, I say, *Esto perpetua!*

She is no longer a wretched colony, returning thanks to her governor for his rapine, and to her king for his oppression; nor is she now a squabbling, fretful sectary, perplexing her little wits, and firing her furious statutes with bigotry, sophistry, disabilities and death, to transmit to posterity insignificance and war …

'Your genius has prevailed. Ireland is now a nation.'

You, with difficulties innumerable, with dangers not a few, have done what your ancestors wished, but could not accomplish; and what your posterity may preserve, but will never equal: you have moulded the jarring elements of your country into a nation. You had not the advantages which were common to other great countries; no monuments, no trophies, none of those outward and visible signs of greatness, such as inspire mankind and connect the ambition of the age which is coming on with the example of that going off, and from the descent and the concatenation of glory: no; you have not had any great act recorded among all your misfortunes, nor have you one public tomb to assemble the crowd, and spread to the living the language of integrity and freedom.

'Spirit of Swift! Spirit of Molyneux!'

Your historians did not supply the want of monuments; on the contrary, these narrators of your misfortunes, who should have felt for your wrongs, and have punished your oppressors with oppressions, natural scourges, the moral indignation of history, compromised with public villainy and trembled; they excited your violence, they suppressed your provocation and wrote in the chain which entrammeled their country. I am come to break that chain, and I congratulate my country, who, without any of the advantages I speak of, going forth, as it were, with nothing but a stone and a sling, and what oppression could not take away, the favour of heaven, accomplished her own redemption, and left you nothing to add and everything to admire.

'*Whatever be the sentence of the court, I am prepared for it.*'

Theobald Wolfe Tone
(1763–98)

Speech at his court martial, Dublin, 10 November 1798

The Williamite settlement of the late 17th century effectively codified a religious pecking order. This gave members of the Church of Ireland full political and economic rights, other Protestant denominations fewer privileges, and Catholics virtually none. Most Patriot politicians who came afterwards, such as Molyneux, Swift and Grattan, were happy enough to maintain this Anglican ascendancy. But a younger generation of middle-class Protestants soon began to argue that 'divide and rule' reinforced British power in Ireland. Theobald Wolfe Tone was their most effective advocate. He wanted 'to break the connection with England, the never-failing source of all our political evils … and to substitute the common name of Irishman in place of the denominations of Catholic, Protestant and Dissenter.'

Tone was among the founder-members of the United Irishmen, a reform club established in Belfast in 1791 and largely Presbyterian in membership. A Dublin Society of United Irishmen was formed a few weeks afterwards. By 1796, the United Irishmen had turned from a political society to military conspirators. An inevitable crackdown followed, prompting Tone to flee the country. He went first to America and on to Paris, where he successfully convinced the revolutionary Directory to support a rising in Ireland. In December 1796, Tone set sail for his homeland with a fleet under Admiral Hoche of 43 ships and some 15,000 men, only to be forced back by rough weather in Bantry Bay.

In the summer of 1798, Tone tried again. A United Irishmen rebellion had broken out sporadically throughout Ireland. France, with less enthusiasm this time, offered some assistance. A contingent of French forces landed in Mayo in August, but only after the rebellion had been put down. Tone himself led some 3000 men to Lough Swilly in Donegal, but was intercepted by British troops on 12 October. He was tried in Dublin wearing his uniform as an adjutant general of the French Navy. Tone was found guilty and sentenced to death by hanging. 'Whatever be the sentence of the court, I am prepared for it,' he defiantly proclaimed in his famous peroration at the trial.

On the morning he was due to be executed, Tone cut his own throat with a penknife, but only succeeded in severing his windpipe. He lingered for a week before dying on 19 November. His body was buried much later in a family plot in Bodenstown, County Kildare, which has since become a shrine of annual pilgrimage for republicans.

BIOGRAPHY

Theobald Wolfe Tone was born in 1763 in Stafford (later Wolfe Tone) Street in Dublin. Like Grattan, he studied at Trinity College, Dublin, and the Middle Temple in London. He came to widespread prominence in 1791 with the publication of an Address on Behalf of the Catholics of Ireland. In the same year he helped to found the United Irishmen in Belfast and Dublin. Following his revolutionary activity and death in 1798, he left a widow, Matilda (with whom he had eloped as a student at Trinity College when she was 16), and a son, William, who published his father's journals and autobiography to acclaim in the United States in the 1820s.

'Whatever be the sentence of the court, I am prepared for it.'

I mean not to give you the trouble of bringing judicial proof to convict me legally of having acted in hostility to the government of his Britannic Majesty in Ireland. I admit the fact. From my earliest youth I have regarded the connection between Great Britain and Ireland as the curse of the Irish nation, and felt convinced that, whilst it lasted, this country could never be free nor happy. My mind has been confirmed in this opinion by the experience of every succeeding year, and the conclusions which I have drawn from every fact before my eyes. In consequence, I was determined to employ all the powers which my individual efforts could move, in order to separate the two countries. That Ireland was not able of herself to throw off the yoke, I knew; I therefore sought for aid wherever it was to be found. In honourable poverty I rejected offers which, to a man in my circumstances, might be considered highly advantageous. I remained faithful to what I thought the cause of my country, and sought in the French Republic an ally to rescue three millions of my countrymen.

'I have laboured to abolish the infernal spirit of religious persecution.'

I believe there is nothing in what remains for me to say which can give any offence; I mean to express my feelings and gratitude towards the Catholic body, in whose cause I was engaged. I have laboured to create a people in Ireland by raising three millions of my countrymen to the rank of citizens. I have laboured to abolish the infernal spirit of religious persecution, by uniting the Catholics and Dissenters. To the former I owe more than ever can be repaid. The services I was so fortunate as to render them they rewarded munificently; but they did more: when the public cry was raised against me – when the friends of my youth swarmed off and left me alone – the Catholics did not desert me; they had the virtue even to sacrifice their own interests to a rigid principle of honour; they refused, though strongly urged, to disgrace a man who, whatever his conduct towards the government might have been, had faithfully and conscientiously discharged his duty towards them; and in so doing, though it was in my own case, I will say they showed an instance of public virtue of which I know not whether there exists another example.

I shall, then, confine myself to some points relative to my connection with the French army. Attached to no party in the French Republic – without interest, without money, without intrigue – the openness and integrity of my views raised me to a high and confidential rank in its armies. I obtained the confidence of the Executive Directory, the approbation of my generals, and I will venture to add, the esteem and affection of my brave comrades. When I review these circumstances, I feel a secret and internal consolation which no reverse of fortune, no sentence in the power of this court to inflict, can deprive me of, or weaken in any degree. Under the flag of the French Republic I originally engaged with a view to save and liberate my own country. For that purpose I have encountered the chances of war amongst strangers; for that purpose I repeatedly braved the terrors of the ocean covered, as I knew it to be, with the triumphant fleets of that power which it was my glory and my duty to oppose. I have sacrificed all my views in life; I have courted poverty; I have left a beloved wife unprotected, and children whom I adored, fatherless. After such a sacrifice, in a cause which I have always considered – conscientiously considered – as the cause of justice and freedom, it is no great effort at this day, to add the sacrifice of my life …

'I have left a beloved wife unprotected, and children whom I adored, fatherless.'

After a combat nobly sustained – a combat which would have excited the respect and sympathy of a generous enemy – my fate has been to become a prisoner to the eternal disgrace of those who gave the orders. I was brought here in irons like a felon. I mention this for the sake of others; for me, I am indifferent to it. I am aware of the fate which awaits me, and scorn equally the tone of complaint and that of supplication. As to the connection between this country and Great Britain, I repeat it – all that has been imputed to me (words, writings and actions), I here deliberately avow. I have spoken and acted with reflection and on principle, and am ready to meet the consequences. Whatever be the sentence of the court, I am prepared for it. Its members will surely discharge their duty – I shall take care not to be wanting in mine.

'*I am sickened with this rant of Irish dignity and independence.*'

John FitzGibbon, Earl of Clare

(1748–1802)

Speech to the House of Lords, Dublin, 10 February 1800

As Ireland grew increasingly restless in the last decades of the 18th century, British opinion concluded that closer ties between the two countries offered the only way to keep the peace. The rebellion of 1798 confirmed this view, and in 1799 the Pitt administration endeavoured to persuade the Irish Parliament to approve a union between Britain and Ireland. This would abolish the Irish Parliament and remove Irish representation to Westminster, but maintain Dublin Castle as the seat of government. This first effort failed. The chief secretary for Ireland, Castlereagh, had underestimated opposition to the union; the following year he was better prepared. Deep pockets helped him pass the Act of Union, which came into effect on 1 January 1801.

On this occasion the bill had been introduced by the lord chancellor, John FitzGibbon, 1st Earl of Clare. A Member of the Dublin Parliament since 1778, his early dalliance with the Patriots had long since ended. By 1800, he had a long-established reputation as the most effective and resolute conservative in Irish politics. FitzGibbon was convinced that only a union of Great Britain and Ireland could preserve Protestant authority while improving life for Catholics. His lengthy speech introducing the Act of Union surveyed Ireland's relationship with Britain over some three centuries.

FitzGibbon was widely detested among the Catholic population. When he died a year after the Union came into force, his funeral was disrupted by protests from a rowdy Dublin mob. More than two centuries later, although often reviled when remembered, he nevertheless enjoys something of a cult status among those who enjoy his intellectual gifts and Olympian self-confidence. Political correctness was not a feature of the 18th century; no one would accuse John FitzGibbon of pandering to the masses.

BIOGRAPHY

John FitzGibbon was born in 1748 and educated at Trinity College, Dublin, Christ Church, Oxford, and the Middle Temple in London. He established a highly lucrative career at the Bar and sat in the Irish House of Commons in 1778–9. Lord chancellor of Ireland from 1789, he was created Earl of Clare in 1795 and subsequently became a British peer with a seat in the House of Lords at Westminster, where he surprisingly failed to prosper. He died a disappointed man in Dublin in January 1802. Although he was widely detested, his children revered his memory. His son John, 2nd Earl of Clare (passionately admired by the young Byron), even fought a duel with Henry Grattan's son on the matter of the first earl's reputation.

*'I am sickened with this rant of Irish dignity
and independence.'*

… But we are told by giving up a separate government, and separate Parliament, we sacrifice national dignity and independence. If gentlemen who enlarge on this theme will talk of their personal dignity and aggrandizement, I can understand them; but when I look at the squalid misery, and profound ignorance, and barbarous manners, and brutal ferocity of the mass of the Irish people, I am sickened with this rant of Irish dignity and independence. Is the dignity and independence of Ireland to consist in the continued depression and unredeemed barbarism of the great majority of the people, and the factious contentions of a puny and rapacious oligarchy, who consider the Irish nation as their political inheritance, and are ready to sacrifice the public peace and happiness to their insatiate love of patronage and power?

'Unless you will civilize your people, it is vain to look for national tranquillity or contentment.'

I hope I feel as becomes a true Irishman, for the dignity and independence of my country, and therefore I would elevate her to her proper station, in the rank of civilized nations. I wish to advance her from the degraded post of a mercenary province, to the proud station of an integral and governing member of the greatest empire in the world. I wish to withdraw the higher orders of my countrymen from the narrow and corrupted sphere of Irish politics, and to direct their attention to objects of national importance, to teach them to improve the natural energies, and extend the resources of their country, to encourage manufacturing, skill and ingenuity, and open useful channels for commercial enterprise; and above all, seriously to exert their best endeavours to tame and civilize the lower orders of the people, to inculcate in them habits of religion and morality, and industry, and due subordination, to relieve their wants, and correct their excesses; unless you will civilize your people, it is vain to look for national tranquillity or contentment.

'Then, and not till then, let my epitaph be written.'

Robert Emmet
(1778–1803)

Speech to the Green Street courthouse, Dublin, 19 September 1803

'Then, and not till then, let my epitaph be written.'

The year 1803 witnessed a pitiful coda to the 1798 rebellion. A group of Dubliners, led by Robert Emmet, endeavoured to stage an uprising to establish Irish independence. Emmet had attempted to re-organize the United Irishmen after 1798. Having amassed arms and procured several private houses around Dublin as depots, he set 23 July as the date for rebellion. The plan was to attack Dublin Castle from nearby Thomas Street. The rebellion – if it can be called that – was a farce. An ill-equipped, drunken mob ran riot through Thomas Street before arrests were made. Emmet managed to escape, heading for the Wicklow hills, but he was captured soon afterwards when visiting his fiancée in Dublin. He was tried and sentenced to death.

The rebellion had been a derisory effort. Yet Emmet managed to join the 'pantheon' of Irish patriots, earning legendary status denied to more important men. His youth, good looks and air of romanticism helped. So did his friendship with the poet Thomas Moore, who immortalized him in a number of popular works. But the most significant contribution to his legend was the peroration at his trial. Nothing became Emmet in life so much as the leaving of it.

Several conflicting versions of his speech were published, including the official court report by William Ridgeway. The most significant discrepancy between them involved the famous conclusion, 'when my country takes her place among the nations of the earth, then, and not till then, let my epitaph be written'. This was absent in the Ridgeway transcript. Some have suggested that nationalist propagandists concocted it. In these latter accounts, Lord Norbury, the presiding judge, was apparently so moved that he burst into tears.

Whatever Emmet actually said, his oration quickly entered popular legend. It was a highlight of the hugely popular book *Speeches from the Dock* (1867). Michael Collins was only one of many able to recite it as a party piece.

BIOGRAPHY

Robert Emmet was born at St Stephen's Green in Dublin in 1778, the youngest son of the viceroy's physician. Active in the Trinity College 'Hist' debating society, he was sent down from the university for his radical politics. After the failed 1798 rebellion, Emmet attempted to re-establish the United Irishmen and to win support in France for an Irish uprising. After his own rising failed in 1803, he fled to the Wicklow mountains, but was captured when visiting his fiancée in a (not as it turned out) safe house in Harold's Cross, Dublin. Emmet was hanged on 20 September 1803 in Thomas Street, the scene of his failed insurrection.

... I have been charged with that importance in the emancipation of my country as to be considered the keystone of the combination of Irishmen; or as your lordship expressed it, 'the life and blood of the conspiracy'. You do me honour overmuch; you have given to the subaltern all the credit of a superior. There are men engaged in this conspiracy who are not only superior to me, but even to your own conceptions of yourself, my lord – men before the splendour of whose genius and virtues I should bow with respectful deference, and who would think themselves disgraced by shaking your bloodstained hand.

'Let no man dare, when I am dead, to charge me with dishonour.'

What, my lord, shall you tell me, on the passage to the scaffold, which that tyranny (of which you are only the intermediary executioner) has erected for my murder, that I am accountable for all the blood that has been and will be shed in this struggle of the oppressed against the oppressor – shall you tell me this, and must I be so very a slave as not to repel it? I do not fear to approach the Omnipotent Judge to answer for the conduct of my whole life; and am I to be appalled and falsified by a mere remnant of mortality here? By you, too, although, if it were possible to collect all the innocent blood that you have shed in your unhallowed ministry in one great reservoir, your lordship might swim in it.

Let no man dare, when I am dead, to charge me with dishonour; let no man attaint my memory, by believing that I could have engaged in any cause but that of my country's liberty and independence; or that I could have become the pliant minion of power, in the oppression and misery of my country. The proclamation of the provisional government speaks for our views; no inference can be tortured from it to countenance barbarity or debasement at home, or subjection, humiliation, or treachery from abroad. I would not have submitted to a foreign oppressor, for the same reason that I would resist the foreign and domestic oppressor. In the dignity of my freedom, I would have fought upon the threshold of my country, and its enemy should enter only by passing over my lifeless corpse. And am I, who lived but for my country, and who have subjected myself to the dangers of the jealous and watchful oppressor, and the bondage of the grave, only to give my countrymen their rights, and my country her independence – am I to be loaded with calumny, and not suffered to resent it? No; God forbid!

'My lords, you are impatient for the sacrifice.'

If the spirits of the illustrious dead participate in the concerns and cares of those who were dear to them in this transitory life, O, ever dear and venerated shade of my

'Then, and not till then, let my epitaph be written.'

departed father! look down with scrutiny upon the conduct of your suffering son, and see if I have, even for a moment, deviated from those principles of morality and patriotism which it was your care to instil into my youthful mind, and for which I am now about to offer up my life.

'I am going to my cold and silent grave – my lamp of life is nearly extinguished.'

My lords, you are impatient for the sacrifice. The blood which you seek is not congealed by the artificial terrors which surround your victim – it circulates warmly and unruffled through the channels which God created for noble purposes, but which you are now bent to destroy for purposes so grievous that they cry to heaven. Be yet patient! I have but a few more words to say – I am going to my cold and silent grave – my lamp of life is nearly extinguished – my race is run – the grave opens to receive me, and I sink into its bosom. I have but one request to ask at my departure from this world; it is – the charity of its silence. Let no man write my epitaph; for, as no man who knows my motives dares now vindicate them, let not prejudice or ignorance asperse them. Let them and me rest in obscurity and peace, and my tomb remain uninscribed, and my memory in oblivion, until other times and other men can do justice to my character. When my country takes her place among the nations of the earth, then, and not till then, let my epitaph be written. I have done.

Sheil addresses the old House of Commons (which burnt down in 1834)

'Hold, I have seen the aliens
do their duty!'

Richard Lalor Sheil
(1791–1851)

Speech to the House of Commons, Westminster, 23 February 1837

'Hold, I have seen the aliens do their duty!'

The dramatist, writer, rabble-rouser and politician Richard Lalor Sheil, though now largely forgotten, was among the most famous Irish personalities of the early 19th century. An active proponent of Catholic relief, he was a sometime associate of Daniel O'Connell, with whom he founded the Catholic Association in 1823. Sheil actively campaigned for Catholic emancipation and proved a captivating speaker. Though not physically prepossessing – he was self-conscious about his lack of height and his high-pitched voice – the content and delivery of his speeches more than compensated. His training as a lawyer helped, as did his study of rhetoric while at Stonyhurst, the Jesuit college in England, and his time as a debater at the Historical Society (the 'Hist') in Trinity College, Dublin. Moreover, in his early years practising law, he had successfully moonlighted as a playwright. This meant his speeches and technique had something of the dramatic about them, utilizing devices of poetry, satire and sentiment to carry a crowd.

Catholic emancipation in 1829 gave Sheil the opportunity to test his rhetorical skills at Westminster. He continued to advocate religious toleration as an MP, observing, 'that men subject to all the duties should be deemed unworthy of the rights of Englishmen appears to me to be a remarkable anomaly'. Sheil rationed his speeches in the House, contributing only when he felt it necessary. This helped make them great occasions, keenly anticipated by fellow MPs. He would spend days preparing and rehearsing an address for maximum impact. Aware of the wider audience away from Westminster, he had an arrangement with the *Morning Chronicle* to publish his speeches afterwards.

The speech to the Commons on 23 February 1837 shows Sheil in full flow. Lord Lyndhurst (lord chancellor in every Tory government between 1827 and 1846) had referred in the House of Lords to the Irish as 'aliens in blood and religion'. Sheil in this reply, which dwelt on the role of Irishmen in fighting for the Empire, prompted furious scenes by pointing directly to Lyndhurst in the gallery. It was unparliamentary behaviour, but wonderful theatre.

A consummate showman and an adept self-publicist, Sheil was nevertheless more than a triumph of style over substance. He was greatly admired by his peers, including those 'mighty opposites' William Gladstone and Benjamin Disraeli.

BIOGRAPHY

Richard Lalor Sheil was born in 1791 in Drumdowney, County Kilkenny, into a prosperous Catholic merchant family, and was educated at Stonyhurst College in Lancashire and at Trinity College, Dublin. Called to the Bar in 1814 at Lincoln's Inn, he failed to secure enough briefs to make a living, and so began writing popular plays, including Adelaide (1814), Bellamira (1818) and Evadne (1819). He became a prominent member of the Catholic Association in the 1820s and, after Catholic emancipation, entered the House of Commons in 1831. Appointed minister to Tuscany in 1850 by the prime minister, Lord John Russell, Sheil died in Florence the following year, just two days after receiving news of the death of his son in Ireland.

... There is one man of great abilities – not a Member of this House, but whose talents and whose boldness have placed him in the topmost place in his party – who, disdaining all imposture, and thinking it the best course to appeal directly to the religious and national antipathies of the people of this country, abandoning all reserve, and flinging off the slender veil by which his political associates affect to cover, although they cannot hide, their motives – distinctly and audaciously tells the Irish people that they are not entitled to the same privileges as Englishmen; and pronounces them, in any particular which could enter his minute enumeration of the circumstances by which fellow citizenship is created, in race, identity and religion, to be aliens – to be aliens in race, to be aliens in country, to be aliens in religion!

Aliens! Good God! Was Arthur, Duke of Wellington, in the House of Lords – and did he not start up and exclaim, 'Hold, I have seen the aliens do their duty!'

'What desperate valour climbed the steeps and filled the moats at Badajos?'

The Duke of Wellington is not a man of an excitable temperament. His mind is of a cast too martial to be easily moved; but, notwithstanding his habitual inflexibility, I cannot help thinking that, when he heard his Roman Catholic countrymen (for we are his countrymen) designated by a phrase as offensive as the abundant vocabulary of his eloquent confederate could supply – I cannot help thinking that he ought to have recollected the many fields of fight in which we have been contributors to his renown. 'The battles, sieges, fortunes that he has passed,' ought to have come back upon him. He ought to have remembered that, from the earliest achievement in which he displayed that military genius which has placed him foremost in the annals of modern warfare, down to that last and surpassing combat which has made his name imperishable – from Assaye to Waterloo – the Irish soldiers, with whom your armies are filled, were the inseparable auxiliaries to the glory with which his unparalleled successes have been crowned.

Whose were the arms that drove your bayonets at Vimiéra through the phalanxes that never reeled in the shock of war before? What desperate valour climbed the steeps and filled the moats at Badajos? All his victories should have rushed and crowded back upon his memory – Vimiéra, Badajos, Salamanca, Albuéra, Toulouse, and, last of all, the greatest. Tell me – for you were there – I appeal to the gallant soldier before me [Sir Henry Harding], from whose opinions I differ, but who bears, I know, a generous heart in an intrepid breast – tell me – for you must needs remember – on that day when the destinies of mankind were trembling in the balance, while death fell in showers, when the artillery of France was levelled with a precision of the most deadly science, when her legions, incited by the voice and inspired by the example of their mighty leader, rushed again and again to the onset – tell me if, for an instant, when to hesitate for an instant was to be lost, the 'aliens' blenched?

'The blood of England, Scotland and of Ireland, flowed in the same stream.'

And when, at length, the moment for the last and decided movement had arrived, and the valour which had so long been wisely checked was, at last, let loose – when, with words familiar, but immortal, the great captain commanded the great assault – tell me if Catholic Ireland with less heroic valour than the natives of this your own glorious country precipitated herself upon the foe? The blood of England, Scotland and of Ireland, flowed in the same stream, and drenched the same field. When the chill morning dawned, their dead lay cold and stark together – in the same deep pit their bodies were deposited; the green corn of spring is now breaking from their commingled dust; the dew falls from heaven upon their union in the grave. Partakers in every peril, in the glory shall we not be permitted to participate; and shall we be told, as a requital, that we are estranged from the noble country for whose salvation our life-blood was poured out?

'Be obedient to me, and Ireland shall be free.'

Daniel O'Connell
(1775–1847)

Speech at Mullaghmast, County Kildare, 1 October 1843

'Be obedient to me, and Ireland shall be free.'

Daniel O'Connell's brand of popular nationalism bequeathed to Ireland an active political culture with a commitment to democracy at its heart. He was a supreme parliamentarian and could muster huge displays of public support away from Westminster. He had used mass backing to drive his campaign for Catholic emancipation in the 1820s, and tried to repeat the trick in the 1840s when facing an unsympathetic Tory administration led by Sir Robert Peel. In 1843 he declared a 'year of repeal' to overturn the Act of Union and reinstate the Irish Parliament.

Around 40 meetings took place that summer across Ireland (except in the northeast). The most notable were held in historic locations, including the seats of the high kings in Tara and at Clontarf, where Brian Boru defeated the Vikings in 1014.

Public support was immense. Hundreds of thousands turned up to hear O'Connell speak. These huge gatherings, dubbed 'monster meetings' by *The Times*, were occasions of great spectacle. O'Connell would arrive in a procession several miles long, accompanied by uniformed bands, floats, local notables and ordinary people. Devotees travelled vast distances to attend.

Despite the numbers involved, meetings always passed off peacefully. O'Connell staked his moral authority on it. He had come of age during a time of revolution at home and abroad. This engendered a lifelong revulsion of violence. Peaceful protest was at the heart of his philosophy and methods. 'There is the same resolution not to violate the peace ... not to give the enemy power by committing a crime,' he said in this 'monster' address at Mullaghmast.

BIOGRAPHY

Daniel O'Connell, known as 'the liberator', was born in 1775 near Cahirciveen, County Kerry, the eldest of ten children. He was adopted at an early age by his uncle Maurice 'Hunting Cap' O'Connell and was later fostered by a local family. He was the driving force behind the campaign for Catholic emancipation in the 1820s. Elected MP for Clare in 1828, O'Connell was unable to take his seat until after emancipation the following year (eventually entering the Commons in 1830). He also led an unsuccessful repeal campaign during the 1840s to re-establish the Irish Parliament. O'Connell died in Genoa in 1847 on his way to Rome and was buried at Glasnevin Cemetery in Dublin. Sackville Street, Dublin's most impressive boulevard, was subsequently renamed O'Connell Street.

O'Connell was helped by the presence of the temperance movement, which ensured that there was no drunkenness to encourage violent behaviour. Good conduct made little impact on the Peel administration, which banned a 'monster meeting' organized for 8 October in Clontarf. O'Connell's decision to comply was consistent with his belief in not courting disturbance, but it marked the beginning of the end for his political authority and popular appeal.

I accept with the greatest alacrity the high honour you have done me in calling me to the chair of this majestic meeting. I feel more honoured than I ever did in my life, with one single exception, and that related to, if possible, an equally majestic meeting at Tara. But I must say that if a comparison were instituted between them, it would take a more discriminating eye than mine to discover any difference between them. There are the same incalculable numbers; there is the same firmness; there is the same determination; there is the same exhibition of love to old Ireland; there is the same resolution not to violate the peace; not to be guilty of the slightest outrage; not to give the enemy power by committing a crime, but peacefully and manfully to stand together in the open day, to protest before man and in the presence of God against the iniquity of continuing the Union.

'The Union is void.'

At Tara I protested against the Union – I repeat the protest at Mullaghmast. I declare solemnly my thorough conviction as a constitutional lawyer, that the Union is totally void in point of principle and of constitutional force. I tell you that no portion of the Empire had the power to traffic on the rights and liberties of the Irish people. The Irish people nominated them to make laws, and not legislatures. They were appointed to act under the Constitution, and not annihilate it. Their delegation from the people was confined within the limits of the Constitution, and the moment the Irish Parliament went beyond those limits and destroyed the Constitution, that moment it annihilated its own power, but could not annihilate the immortal spirit of liberty which belongs, as a rightful inheritance, to the people of Ireland. Take it, then, from me that the Union is void.

I admit there is the force of a law, because it has been supported by the policeman's truncheon, by the soldier's bayonet and by the horseman's sword; because it is supported by the courts of law and those who have power to adjudicate in them; but I say solemnly, it is not supported by constitutional right. The Union, therefore, in my thorough conviction, is totally void, and I avail myself of this opportunity to announce to several hundreds of thousands of my fellow subjects that the Union is an unconstitutional law and that it is not fated to last long – its hour is approaching…

O my friends, I will keep you clear of all treachery – there shall be no bargain, no compromise with England – we shall take nothing but repeal, and a Parliament in College Green. You will never, by my advice, confide in any false hopes they hold out to you; never confide in anything coming from them, or cease from your struggle, no matter what promise may be held to you, until you hear me say I am satisfied; and I will tell you where I will say that – near the statue of King William, in College Green. No; we came here to express our determination to die to a man, if necessary, in the cause of old Ireland. We came to take advice of each other, and, above all, I believe you came here to take my advice. I can tell you, I have the game in my hand – I have the triumph secure – I have the repeal certain, if you but obey my advice.

I will go slow – you must allow me to do so – but you will go sure. No man shall find himself imprisoned or persecuted who follows my advice. I have led you thus far in safety; I have swelled the multitude of repealers until they are identified with the entire population, or nearly the entire population, of the land, for seven-eighths of the Irish people are now enrolling themselves repealers. I do not want more power; I have power enough; and all I ask of you is to allow me to use it. I will go on quietly and slowly, but I will go on firmly, and with a certainty of success ...

'Starlight sparkling from the eye of a Kildare beauty.'

If there is any one here who is for the Union, let him say so. Is there anybody here for the repeal? (*Cries of 'All, all!'*) Yes, my friends, the Union was begot in iniquity – it was perpetuated in fraud and cruelty. It was no compact, no bargain, but it was an act of the most decided tyranny and corruption that was ever yet perpetrated. Trial by jury was suspended – the right of personal protection was at an end – courts martial sat throughout the land – and the County of Kildare, among others, flowed with blood. We shall stand peaceably side by side in the face of every enemy. Oh, how delighted was I in the scenes which I witnessed as I came along here today! How my heart throbbed, how my spirit was elevated, how my bosom swelled with delight at the multitude which I beheld, and which I shall behold, of the stalwart and strong men of Kildare! I was delighted at the activity and force that I saw around me, and my old heart grew warm again in admiring the beauty of the dark-eyed maids and matrons of Kildare. Oh, there is a starlight sparkling from the eye of a Kildare beauty that is scarcely equalled, and could not be excelled, all over the world. And remember that you are the sons, the fathers, the brothers, and the husbands of such women, and a traitor or a coward could never be connected with any of them. Yes, I am in a county, remarkable in the history of Ireland for its bravery and its misfortune, for its credulity in the faith of others, for its people judged of the Saxon by the honesty and honour of their own natures. I am in a county celebrated for the sacredness of shrines and fanes. I am in a county where the lamp of Kildare's holy shrine burned with its sacred fire, through ages of darkness and storm – that fire which for six centuries burned before the high altar without being extinguished, being fed continuously, without the slightest interruption, and it seemed to me to have been not an inapt representation of the continuous fidelity and religious love of country of the men of Kildare.

You have those high qualities – religious fidelity, continuous love of country. Even your enemies admit that the world has never produced any people that exceeded the Irish in activity and strength. The Scottish philosopher has declared, and the French philosopher has confirmed it, that number one in the human race is, blessed be heaven, the Irishman. In moral virtue, in religion, in perseverance, and in glorious temperance, you excel. Have I any teetotallers here? Yes, it is teetotalism that is repealing the Union. I could not afford to bring you together, I would not dare to bring you together, but that I had the teetotallers for my police.

Yes, among the nations of the earth, Ireland stands number one in the physical strength of her sons and in the beauty and purity of her daughters. Ireland, land of my forefathers, how my mind expands, and my spirit walks abroad in something of majesty, when I contemplate the high qualities, inestimable virtues and true purity and piety and religious fidelity of the inhabitants of your green fields and productive mountains. Oh, what a scene surrounds us! It is not only the countless thousands of brave and active and peaceable and religious men that are here assembled, but Nature herself has written her character with the finest beauty in the verdant plains that surround us.

'O my friends, it is a country worth fighting for.'

Let any man run around the horizon with his eye, and tell me if created nature ever produced anything so green and so lovely, so undulating, so teeming with production. The richest harvests that any land can produce are those reaped in Ireland; and then here are the sweetest meadows, the greenest fields, the loftiest mountains, the purest streams, the noblest rivers, the most capacious harbours – and her water power is equal to turn the machinery of the whole world. O my friends, it is a country worth fighting for – it is a country worth dying for; but, above all, it is a country worth being tranquil, determined, submissive and docile for; disciplined as you are in obedience to those who are breaking the way, and trampling down the barriers between you and your constitutional liberty, I will see every man of you having a vote, and every man protected by the ballot from the agent or landlord. I will see labour protected, and every title to possession recognized, when you are industrious and honest. I will see prosperity again throughout your land – the busy hum of the shuttle and the tinkling of the smithy shall be heard again. We shall see the nailer employed even until the middle of the night, and the carpenter covering himself with his chips. I will see prosperity in all its gradations spreading through a happy, contented, religious land. I will hear the hymn of a happy people go forth at sunrise to God in praise of His mercies – and I will see the evening sun set down among the uplifted hands of a religious and free population. Every blessing that man can bestow and religion can confer upon the faithful heart shall spread throughout the land. Stand by me – join with me – I will say be obedient to me, and Ireland shall be free.

'*Gentlemen, you have a country!*'

Thomas Davis
(1814–45)

Speech at The University of Dublin, Trinity College, published 17 June 1839

Thomas Davis represented a new kind of nationalism. Unlike previous Protestant nationalists, such as the Patriots or those in the United Irishmen, Davis was as interested in culture as in economics and sovereignty. This was something that he and his comrades in Young Ireland shared with romantic movements across Europe. It was a nationalism based on poetry, music and a common history as much as religion or politics. Education was the key to advancing this agenda. His best known exhortation – 'educate that you may be free' – has guided Irish educators and nationalists ever since.

The issue of education in Davis's time (no less than now) was highly complex. Both the Catholic Church and the Church of Ireland demanded that it be provided along denominational lines. Matters were complicated by the fact that Ireland had just one university, Trinity College, which was entirely Protestant in its foundation and had only a small number of Catholic students. Catholics were campaigning vigorously to establish their own university, yet for Davis this was an anathema. He spoke out against the establishment of new denominational institutions much as he railed about the stultifying monoculture of Trinity. For Davis, education was the means to bring people of different denominations together not keep them apart.

As a student in Trinity himself, Davis had been frustrated by the character of the university, which he found self-satisfied and out of touch with the majority of Irish society. Intellectual fulfilment came through debates at the 'Hist' debating society. Robert Emmet and Richard Lalor Sheil were among his eminent predecessors. He later recalled that it was at the 'Hist' that he developed his ideas on nationalism and independence. In 1839 he delivered this precociously brilliant address on the importance of the debating society as an instrument of change. Students, he urged, should look beyond the curriculum laid out by professors to educate themselves in preparation for playing a full role in the life of the nation. It is an idea that endures.

> **BIOGRAPHY**
>
> **Thomas Davis** was born in Mallow, County Cork, in 1814 and educated at Trinity College, Dublin, where he established a precocious reputation as a nationalist thinker. He joined the Repeal Association in 1840, but clashed with O'Connell about denominational education. With John Blake Dillon and Charles Gavan Duffy, he founded *The Nation* newspaper in 1842, espousing a romantic nationalism based on a common Irish identity. Journalists dubbed the friends 'Young Ireland' and the name stuck. Davis died from scarlet fever aged just 31. He was buried in Mount Jerome Cemetery after a funeral that was a major public event.

‛ … Gentlemen, the Dublin University is the laughing stock of the literary world, and an obstacle to the nation's march; its inaccessible library, 'the mausoleum of literature' and effete system of instruction (with the exception in favour of the medical and surgical school) render it ridiculous abroad; add its unaccounted funds, and its bigot laws, and know why it is hated…

'Patriotism is human philanthropy.'

But, gentlemen, you have a country! The people among whom we were born, with whom we live, for whom, if our minds are in health, we have most sympathy, or those over whom we have power – power to make them wise, great, good. Reason points out our native land as the field for our exertions, and tells us that without patriotism a profession of benevolence is the cloak of the selfish man; and does not sentiment confirm the decree of reason? The country of our birth, our education, of our recollections, ancestral, personal, national; the country of our loves, our friendships, our hopes; our country: the cosmopolite is unnatural, base – I would fain say, impossible. To act on a world is for those above it, not of it. Patriotism is human philanthropy.

Gentlemen, many of you possess, more of you are growing into the possession of, great powers – powers which were given you for good, which you may use for evil. I trust that not as adventurers, or rash meddlers, will you enter on public life. But to enter on it in some way or other the state of mind in Ireland will compel you. You must act as citizens, and it is well, *'non nobis solum nati sumus, ortusque nostri partem patria vindicat.'* ['We are not born for ourselves alone but our country claims a share of our being.' Plato, quoted by Cicero in *De Officiis*, Book One.] Patriotism once felt to be a duty becomes so. To act in politics is a matter of duty everywhere; here, of necessity. To make that action honourable to yourselves, and serviceable to your country, is a matter of choice. In your public career you will be solicited by a thousand temptations to sully your souls with the gold and place of a foreign court, or the transient breath of a dishonest popularity; dishonest, when adverse to the good, though flattering to the prejudices of the people …

'Happiness is at hand.'

But if neither the present nor the past can rouse you, let the sun of hope, the beams of the future, awake you to exertion in the cause of patriotism. Seek, oh seek to make your country not behind at least in the progress of the nations. Education, the apostle of progress, hath gone forth. Knowledge is not virtue, but may be rendered its precursor. Virtue is not alone enjoyment, is not all happiness; but be sure, when the annunciation of virtue comes, the advent of happiness is at hand. Seek to take your country forward in her progress to that goal, where she, in common with the other nations, may hear that annunciation of virtue, and share that advent of happiness, holiness, and peace.

*'Eternity is not long enough,
nor hell hot enough.'*

David Moriarty
(1814–77)

Address in St Mary's Cathedral, Killarney, County Kerry, 17 February 1867

'Eternity is not long enough, nor hell hot enough.'

The Irish Republican Brotherhood or IRB (often called the Fenians) was a revolutionary movement formed in 1858. Based in the United States (particularly New York) and active across Ireland, this secret society organized itself into tight-knit local cells to prevent infiltration by British spies. This concealment, along with its nationalistic and revolutionary aims, made the IRB a target for the Catholic hierarchy. The church across Europe had sought to stem the rise of militant nationalism, not least after the travails of Pius IX in 1848 at the hands of Mazzini in Italy. The fact that the cardinal archbishop of Dublin, Paul Cullen, had witnessed Mazzini's men chase the pope from Rome now made him all the more determined to resist a similar 'compound of folly and wickedness' in Ireland.

Cullen's detestation of the Fenians was as nothing compared to that of David Moriarty, bishop of Kerry. On 12 February 1867, an armed group of 35 Fenian sympathizers launched a cackhanded rebellion in his diocese. Their ambitious aim was to bring down the entire British Empire. Moriarty was outraged. At mass the following Sunday, he delivered this furious attack from the pulpit excoriating the rebels. His assertion that 'eternity is not long enough, nor hell hot enough to punish such miscreants' quickly became infamous. His main target, however, was not the rank and file Fenians who had engaged in the rebellion itself, but rather the American-based revolutionaries who had stirred up sedition from across the Atlantic. These men had 'lost the Irish character', were 'not our people' and 'care not how many are murdered'.

In differentiating between the Irish at home and those abroad, Moriarty had identified a vital discourse with the diaspora. It was one replete with threats for some and opportunities for others.

BIOGRAPHY

David Moriarty was born at Derryvrin in County Kerry in 1814, and was educated in France and at St Patrick's College, Maynooth. Appointed bishop of Kerry in 1856, he was a powerful speaker, who was often called upon by the Catholic hierarchy to preach at important church events. Although he had been an admirer of Thomas Davis and Young Ireland, he opposed the Fenians and was suspicious of the home rule movement. He was a friend and confidant of John Henry Newman and argued at the First Vatican Council that it was inopportune to define papal infallibility (although he subsequently accepted the doctrine). Moriarty died in 1877 and was buried at St Mary's Cathedral, Killarney.

'My dear Brethren – it is the duty of the pastor of a diocese to give advice and correction when his flock have been led into any extraordinary folly, and to reprove and rebuke them if they have perpetrated any extraordinary crime. It is also his duty, if they suffer unmerited disgrace, to justify them as far as he is able. Now, since we met here last Sunday, some people in Kerry have been betrayed into an act of madness … It would seem that some dozen [lunatics] left the town of Cahirciveen on Wednesday evening with the avowed object of making war on the Queen of England, and of upsetting the British Empire. I think there is not one inmate of the asylum who would not hold his side for laughter if he heard it. Now, if this were only folly we might be satisfied to deplore it, but these people were answerable to God for their conduct, for they, I regret to say, had sense enough to know what they were doing is a grievous crime. It is just 12 months ago since I explained at considerable length in my last Lenten pastoral the deep guiltiness of rebellion against lawful authority, so they cannot plead that they were not instructed and forewarned. They resisted the ordinance of God, and by so doing, they purchased for themselves damnation …

'They have lost the Irish character in the cities of America.'

One word about the prime movers of all this mischief. If we must condemn the foolish youth who have joined in this conspiracy, how much must we not execrate the conduct of those designing villains who have been entrapping innocent youth, and organizing the work of crime. Thank God they are not our people, or if they ever were, they have lost the Irish character in the cities of America; but beyond them there are criminals of a far deeper guilt. The men, while they send their dupes into danger, are fattening on the spoils in Paris and New York. The execrable swindlers who care not to endanger the necks of the men who trust, who care not how many are murdered by the rebel or hanged by the strong arm of the law, provided they can get a supply of dollars either for their pleasures or their wants. O God's heaviest curse, His withering, blasting, blighting curse is on them. I preached to you last Sunday on the eternity of Hell's torments. Human reason was inclined to say – 'it is a hard word and who can bear it'. But when we look down into the fathomless depth of this infamy of the heads of the Fenian conspiracy, we must acknowledge that eternity is not long enough, nor hell hot enough to punish such miscreants.

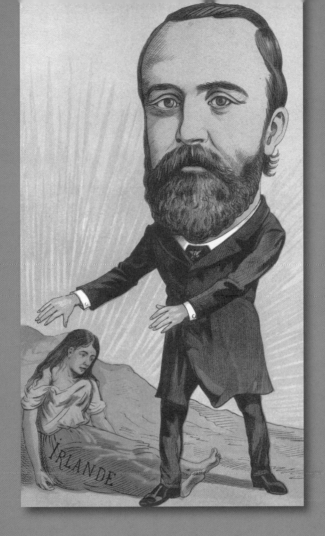

'No man has the right to fix the boundary to the march of a nation.'

Charles Stewart Parnell
(1846–91)

Speech in Cork, 21 January 1885

By the early 1880s, politicians of all colours recognized that Charles Stewart Parnell was a potential kingmaker at Westminster. He had already successfully woven the strands of land agitation, Fenianism and constitutional politics to a point where the Irish Party exerted considerable influence in the House of Commons. In 1882, he had focused his attention on home rule. By 1885 this was achieving results. A general election was in the offing. Coercive legislation to quell the agrarian disturbances associated with the land war had just expired. The government calculated that buying off the Home Rule Party would keep Ireland sweet at a politically sensitive time. Joseph Chamberlain, liberalism's most innovative politician, proposed Irish self-government based around a 'central board'. This was in essence local government writ large, with provision for greater autonomy in areas such as education and communications.

Chamberlain had put more on the table than any minister before him, but the scheme fell well short of what most people recognised as 'home rule' (vague though that notion was). Parnell had no problem with Chamberlain's proposals *per se*, but he could not accept them as a final settlement. He articulated this opposition at a rallying address to constituents in Cork in 1885. It was an inspirational yet purposely imprecise declaration of intent. As the historian Alan O'Day notes, 'besides being an affirmation of national identity, Parnell's speech was tactically astute, managing the near impossible task of satisfying almost everyone, while giving no clue as to any specific reform priorities, or clarification of what he meant by home rule other than citing Grattan's Parliament as the limit of the demand possible under the British constitution. The speech was an unparalleled case of Parnell's infinite capacity to mix mundane realism with uplifting sentiments.' The tactic paid off. During the course of 1885, the British prime minister, William Gladstone, 'converted' to home rule and introduced a bill the following year.

Parnell's observation in this speech that 'no man has the right to fix the boundary to the march of a nation ... ' became his own epitaph. His successor, John Redmond, chose it as the legend to be inscribed on the Parnell monument erected in Dublin's Sackville (later O'Connell) Street.

BIOGRAPHY

Charles Stewart Parnell was born into a Protestant family at Avondale, County Wicklow in 1846 and named after his maternal grandfather, Charles Stewart – an American naval hero. Becoming MP for Meath in 1875, he took up the leadership of the Home Rule Party four years later. Parnell forged the powerful alliance ('the new departure') between the Land League and supporters of home rule that helped put the Irish question at the heart of British politics. Despite fame as 'the uncrowned king of Ireland', he remained a deeply private man. 'It is a joke among his intimates that to Mr Parnell the being Parnell does not exist,' wrote the home rule MP and journalist, T.P. O'Connor. He died in October 1891, just a few short months after marrying Katharine O'Shea at Steyning register office.

*'No man has the right to fix the boundary to
the march of a nation.'*

... At the election in 1880 I laid certain principles before you and you accepted them (*applause, and cries of 'we do'*). I said and I pledged myself, that I should form one of an independent Irish party to act in opposition to every English government which refused to concede the just rights of Ireland (*applause*). And the longer time which is gone by since then, the more I am convinced that that is the true policy to pursue so far as parliamentary policy is concerned, and that it will be impossible for either or both of the English parties to contend for any long time against a determined band of Irishmen acting honestly upon these principles, and backed by the Irish people (*cheers*).

'Do what is beyond your strength even should you fail sometimes.'

But we have not alone had that object view – we have always been very careful not to fetter or control the people at home in any way, not to prevent them from doing anything by their own strength which it is possible for them to do. Sometimes, perhaps, in our anxiety in this direction we have asked them to do what is beyond their strength, but I hold that it is better even to encourage you to do what is beyond your strength even should you fail sometimes in the attempt than to teach you to be subservient and unreliant (*applause*). You have been encouraged to organize yourselves, to depend upon the rectitude of your cause for your justification, and to depend upon the determination which has helped Irishmen through many centuries to retain the name of Ireland and to retain her nationhood.

Nobody could point to any single action of ours in the House of Commons or out of it which was not based upon the knowledge that behind us existed a strong and brave people, that without the help of the people our exertions would be as nothing, and that with their help and with their confidence we should be, as I believe we shall prove to be in the near future, invincible and unconquerable (*great applause*) ...

'Without the help of the people our exertions would be as nothing.'

I come back – and every Irish politician must be forcibly driven back – to the consideration of the great question of National Self-Government for Ireland (*cheers*). I do not know how this great question will be eventually settled. I do not know whether England will be wise in time and concede to constitutional arguments and methods the restitution of that which was stolen from us towards the close of the last century (*cheers*). It is given to none of us to forecast the future, and just as it is impossible for us to say in what way or by what means the National question may be settled, in what way full justice may be done to Ireland, so it is impossible for us to say to what extent that justice should be done. We cannot ask for less than restitution of Grattan's Parliament (*renewed cheering*). But no man has the right to fix the boundary to the march of a nation (*great cheers*). No man has a right to say to his country, 'Thus far shalt thou go, and no further'; and we have never attempted to fix the *ne plus ultra* to the progress of Ireland's nationhood, and we never shall (*cheers*).

'We shall not give up anything which the future may put in favour of our country.'

But gentlemen, while we leave those things to time, circumstances and the future, we must each one of us resolve in our own hearts that we shall at all times do everything which within us lies to obtain for Ireland the fullest measure of her rights (*applause*). In this way we shall avoid difficulties and contentions amongst each other. In this way we shall not give up anything which the future may put in favour of our country, and while we struggle today for that which may seem possible for us with our combination, we must struggle for it with the proud consciousness, and that we shall not do anything to hinder or prevent better men who may come after us from gaining better things than those for which we now contend (*prolonged applause*).

'The Land League repels the accusation, and counter-charges landlordism.'

Michael Davitt
(1846–1906)

Speech to the Special Irish Commission, 29 October 1889

The assassination by the Invincibles (an extremist nationalist group) of the chief secretary of Ireland, Lord Frederick Cavendish, and Thomas Burke, permanent undersecretary at the Irish office, in Phoenix Park in May 1882 was the most daring and savage act of political violence seen in 19th-century Ireland. At the time, Charles Stewart Parnell had been trying to dampen revolutionary tendencies. It had seemed momentarily that the murders would put him at a significant political disadvantage, but his wholehearted condemnation of the killings proved sufficient to appease British public opinion.

Some years later, however, rumours began to spread in Tory circles that Parnell's denunciation had been cant. On 7 March 1887 *The Times* published the first in a series of articles on 'Parnellism and Crime' that put these rumours into the public domain. The political motive was clear. The newspaper announced that its object was 'to remind the public of certain facts connected with the home rule agitation, which are too often permitted to drop out of sight'. The articles accused Parnell of having written to the Phoenix Park murderers expressing his support and assuring them that his condemnation of their actions had been disingenuous. They also dealt at length with Michael Davitt and the Land League, which it was claimed had run a campaign of murder during the land war (the agrarian agitation that had begun in rural Ireland during the 1870s). A connection was alleged between the Fenians (of which Davitt was a member) and the Invincibles.

BIOGRAPHY

Michael Davitt was born in County Mayo in 1846 during the Great Irish Famine. His family were evicted from their home in 1850 and moved to England. At nine years old, he began working in a mill, where he lost an arm in an accident. Ironically, this was the making of him: the misfortune allowed Davitt to attend a Wesleyan school and later the Mechanics' Institute, where he came under the influence of veteran Chartist leader, Ernest Jones. He joined the Fenians in 1865, which led to him being found guilty of treason-felony in 1870. After seven years' hard labour, he was released on licence in 1877 and returned to Ireland to found the Land League in Mayo. Davitt was pivotal in bringing together Parnell and the Fenians. He died in Dublin of blood poisoning in 1906 and was buried at Straide, County Mayo.

The government established a special inquiry in 1887 to investigate these accusations. A commission sat for two years and was widely reported upon around the world. In February 1889, Richard Pigott, a star witness for *The Times*, was dramatically exposed under cross-examination as having forged the 'Parnell' letters. Parnell was effectively vindicated. Pigott fled to Madrid, where he committed suicide.

The commission's report was published in 1890. It cleared Davitt, saying that while he was engaged in a conspiracy to bring about the separation of Britain and Ireland, his disapproval of 'crime and outrage' had been *bona fide*. Davitt's

*'The Land League repels the accusation, and
counter-charges landlordism.'*

speech to the commission ran for five days and combined a rational defence of the Land League with a counterattack on landlordism. It offered an eloquent example of how the Irish in public life cleverly manipulated the institutions and language of the Victorian state to make a case for reform in Ireland.

... I may be wrong in my opinion, but I thought and believed that if one with my record of suffering, physical and otherwise, at the hands of Irish landlordism and Castle rule; of the conflict of a lifetime with the law as it has been administered in Ireland, and of the punishment which that conflict has entailed: I felt and believed if I came before this tribunal and pleaded, in my own way, the cause of the Celtic peasantry of Ireland, that perhaps the story which I have told and the case which I have submitted might possibly, in part or in whole, arrest the attention of the people of Great Britain when they come to study your lordships' labours and report.

And I thought and hoped that in the defence which I have made there might possibly be found some help in the task of finally solving this Anglo-Irish struggle. Should my hope be realized, should I have contributed but in the least possible degree to point to a just and feasible solution of a problem which would bring peace and some chance of prosperity to Ireland, I shall be happy in the recollection of the task which I am now bringing to a close.

'Distrust and opposition and bitter recollections will die out of the Irish heart.'

I can only say that I represent the working classes of my country here as I did in the Land League movement, and I know they feel, as I do, that, no matter how bitter past memories have rankled in our hearts, no matter how much we have suffered in the past in person or in our country's cause, no matter how fiercely some of us have fought against and denounced the injustice of alien misgovernment: I know that, before a feeling of kindness and of good will on the part of the people of England, Scotland and Wales, and in a belief in their awakening sense of justice toward our country, all distrust and opposition and bitter recollections will die out of the Irish heart, and the Anglo-Irish strife will terminate forever when landlordism and Castle rule are dethroned by Great Britain's verdict for reason and for right.

My lords, I now bring my observations to a close. Whatever legal points are to occupy your lordships' study and care in this long and arduous investigation, it will appear to the public, who will study the report or the decision of this tribunal, that two institutions stood indicted before it.

One has had a life of centuries, the other an existence of but a few brief years. They are charged, respectively, by the accused and the accusers, with the responsibility for the agrarian crimes of the period covered by this inquiry.

'Nor have I … had to scour the purlieus of American cities for men who would sell evidence.'

One is Irish landlordism, the other is the Irish Land League. *The Times* alleges that the younger institution is the culprit. The Land League, through me, its founder, repels the accusation, and counter-charges landlordism with being the instigation and the cause, not alone of the agrarian violence and crimes from 1879 to 1887, but of all which are on record, from the times spoken of by Spenser and Davis in the days of Elizabeth down to the date of this commission.

To prove this real and hoary-headed culprit guilty I have not employed or purchased the venal talent of a forger, or offered the tempting price of liberty for incriminatory evidence to unhappy convicts in penal cells. Neither have I brought convicted assassins or professional perjurers before your lordships. I have not sought assistance such as this with which to sustain my case. Nor have I … had to scour the purlieus of American cities for men who would sell evidence that might repair the case which Richard Pigott's confession destroyed, and which his self-inflicted death has sealed with tragic emphasis.

'The Isle of Destiny.'

But there is another and a higher interest involved in the drama of this commission now rapidly drawing to a close; an interest far surpassing in importance, and the possible consequences of your lordships' judgment, anything else comprised in this investigation. It stands between *The Times* and landlordism on the one hand; the persons here charged and the Land League on the other. In bygone ages historians, with some prophetic instinct, called it 'The Isle of Destiny'.

And Destiny seems to have reserved it for a career of trial, of suffering, and of sorrow. That same Destiny has linked this country close to England. Politically it has remained there for 700 years or more. During that period few people ever placed upon this earth have experienced more injustice or more criminal neglect at the hands of their rulers than we have.

This even English history will not and dare not deny. This land so tried and treated has nevertheless struggled, generation after generation, now with one means, now with another, to widen the sphere of its contracted religious, social and political

'*The Land League repels the accusation, and
counter-charges landlordism.*'

liberties – liberties so contracted by the deliberate policy of its English governing power; and ever and always were these struggles made against the prejudice and might, and often the cruelties, of this same power, backed by the support or the indifference of the British nation.

But despite all this, the cause so fought and upheld has ever and always succeeded, sooner or later, in vindicating its underlying principles of truth and justice, and in winning from the power which failed to crush them an after-justification of their righteous demands.

'*Put force and mistrust away.*'

A people so persevering in its fight for the most priceless and most cherished of human and civil rights, so opposed, but so invariably vindicated, might surely in these days of progress and of enlightenment excite in the breasts of Englishmen other feelings than those of jealousy, hate, revenge and fear. To many, thank God, it has appealed successfully at last to what is good and what is best in English nature. It has spoken to the spirit of Liberty, and has turned the love of justice in the popular mind toward Ireland, and has asked the British people, in the interests of peace, to put force and mistrust away with every other abandoned weapon of Ireland's past misrule, and to place in their stead the soothing and healing remedies of confidence and friendship, based upon reason and equality …

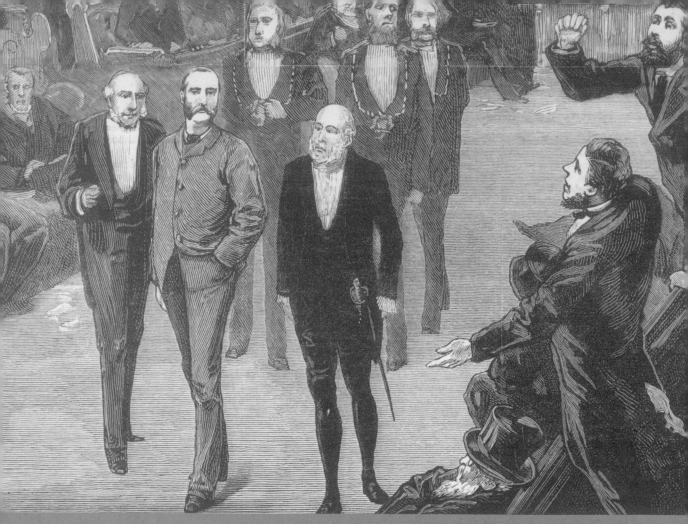

Parnell (centre) being escorted from the House of Commons

'Parnell, by his public misconduct, has utterly disqualified himself.'

The Catholic hierarchy

Letter read in Catholic churches across Ireland, 3 July 1891

'Parnell, by his public misconduct, has utterly disqualified himself.'

C.S. Parnell was the greatest figure in Irish politics since Daniel O'Connell. If it was a cliché to describe him as the uncrowned king of Ireland, it was true nonetheless. The transformation in the fortunes of the home rule movement under his leadership can scarcely be exaggerated. He took a loose grouping of parliamentarians and turned them into a powerful disciplined force. His alliance with the land agitators and Fenians bolstered the party's popularity in Ireland. By 1890 he had succeeded in putting government for Ireland firmly on the British political agenda, and while the first home rule bill had faltered in Westminster it remained a live issue.

Parnell was a profoundly complex individual. Aloof and unclubbable, he had nevertheless found genuine happiness in a relationship with Katharine ('Kitty') O'Shea. The two met in the summer of 1880 and were both struck by a *coup de foudre*. Katharine was estranged from her husband, William O'Shea, MP for Clare. Parnell and Katharine eventually entered into a *de facto* marriage, living as man and wife and having two daughters together. The liaison was common knowledge in political circles. Katharine's husband – the kind of man that Victorians described as a bounder – took advantage of the situation to get preferment. But in 1890, down on his luck and having lost his parliamentary seat, O'Shea petitioned his wife for divorce. Parnell was cited as co-respondent. On 17 November the court handed down a verdict in William's favour.

Public opinion was scandalized. Gladstone's Nonconformist supporters throughout Britain pressurized him to withdraw support for Parnell. It was this prospect of losing Liberal backing more than Parnell's behaviour itself that turned many in the Irish parliamentary party against him. In Ireland the Catholic hierarchy condemned Parnell, pronouncing him 'unfit for leadership'. In the months that followed, the Irish leader fought for his reputation and political career. The results of three by-elections saw Parnellite candidates soundly beaten. In each campaign, Parnell came up against the Catholic clergy, who resolutely supported the opposing candidates. It was prior to the by-election in Carlow on 7 July 1891 that the Catholic church released an address to be read from the pulpit by local priests. It stated unambiguously that Parnell had 'utterly disqualified himself' to be leader of the Home Rule Party.

The Parnellite controversy tore Irish politics apart for more than a decade. Lingering resentment about the scandal was brilliantly depicted in James Joyce's evocation of turn-of-the-century Dublin, *Portrait of the Artist as a Young Man*. As Mr Casey observes, it was 'the priests and the priests' pawns [who] broke Parnell's heart and hounded him into his grave'.

'Parnell, by his public misconduct, has utterly disqualified himself to be the political leader.'

We, the Archbishops and Bishops of Ireland, assembled in general meeting for the first time since the issuing of the declaration of our standing committee last December, hereby record the solemn expression of our judgment as pastors of the Irish people that Mr Parnell, by his public misconduct, has utterly disqualified himself to be the political leader, that since the issuing of that declaration Mr Parnell's public action and that of his recognized agents and organs in the press, especially their open hostility to ecclesiastical authority, has supplied new and convincing proof that he is wholly unworthy of the confidence of Catholics, and we therefore feel bound on this occasion to call on our people to repudiate his leadership.

Signed by all the Archbishops and Bishops with the exception of Most Rev. Dr O'Dwyer, Bishop of Limerick.

'His heart still yearned toward the people of Ireland.'

John Dillon
(1851–1927)

Speech to the House of Commons, Westminster, 20 May 1898

Since the Act of Union in 1801, politicians from Ireland had endeavoured with limited success to convince British MPs of the need for Irish self-government. This changed in 1885 when Gladstone – 'as fast bound to Ireland as Ulysses was to his mast' – converted to home rule. His earlier administration had already disestablished the Church of Ireland and begun the process of land reform. In 1886 and again in 1893 he introduced bills to give Ireland home rule. Each attempt ended in failure. Yet while Gladstone was sympathetic to Ireland, many Irish MPs were less well-disposed to him. It was, after all, Gladstone (himself subject to gossip about his private life) who had caved to Nonconformist pressure to demand that the Home Rule Party drop Parnell in the wake of the O'Shea divorce scandal. That ultimatum had split Parnell's party and his country.

John Dillon was one of the Home Rule MPs who sided against Parnell, so it was unsurprising that this tribute on the death of Gladstone in 1898 should have been so warm. His praise for Gladstone's service to Ireland spoke for that body of Irish opinion, perhaps the majority, symbolized by the truism that 'every' house in Ireland contained a picture of the 'Grand Old Man'.

Dillon continued to sit at Westminster until 1918, when he lost his seat in East Mayo to Éamon de Valera. The Dillon name thrived in Free State politics through his son, James, who became one of independent Ireland's finest parliamentary orators.

BIOGRAPHY

John Dillon was born in 1851 in Blackrock, County Dublin, son of the Young Irelander John Blake Dillon. He was educated privately and at the medical school of the Catholic University in Dublin (later University College Dublin), where he was auditor of the Literary and Historical Society. Despite an early devotion to Parnell, he became chairman of the anti-Parnellites at Westminster in 1886. He briefly led the Irish Party in 1918 following the death of John Redmond, but retired from politics after losing his seat to Sinn Féin later that year. His son, James, served as a minister in two governments in independent Ireland. Dillon died in London on 4 August 1927.

As an Irishman I feel that I have a special right to join in paying a tribute to the great Englishman who died yesterday, because the last and, as all men will agree, the most glorious years of his strenuous and splendid life were dominated by the love which he bore to our nation, and by the eager and even passionate desire to serve Ireland and give her liberty and peace.

By virtue of the splendid quality of his nature, which seemed to give him perpetual youth, Mr Gladstone's faith in a cause to which he had once devoted himself never wavered, nor did his enthusiasm grow cold. Difficulties and the weight of advancing years were alike ineffectual to blunt the edge of his purpose or to daunt his splendid courage, and even when racked with pain, and when the shadow of death was darkening over him, his heart still yearned toward the people of Ireland, and his last public utterance was a message of sympathy for Ireland and of hope for her future. His was a great and deep nature. He loved the people with a wise and persevering love. His love of the people and his abiding faith in the efficacy of liberty and of government based on the consent of the people, as an instrument of human progress, was not the outcome of youthful enthusiasm, but the deep-rooted growth of long years, and drew its vigour from an almost unparalleled experience of men and of affairs. Above all men I have ever known or read of, in his case the lapse of years seemed to have influence to narrow his sympathies or to contract his heart. Young men felt old beside him. And to the last no generous cause, no suffering people, appealed to him in vain, and that glorious voice which had so often inspirited the friends of freedom and guided them to victory was the last at the service of the weak and the oppressed of whatever race or nation. Mr Gladstone was the greatest Englishman of his time.

'The people of this island are joined in their sorrow by many peoples.'

He loved his own people as much as any Englishman that ever lived. But through communion with the hearts of his own people he acquired that wider and greater gift – the power of understanding and sympathizing with other peoples. He entered into their sorrows and felt for their oppressions. And with splendid courage he did not hesitate, even in the case of his much-loved England, to condemn her when he thought she was wronging others, and in so doing he fearlessly faced odium and unpopularity among his own people, which it must have been bitter for him to bear; and so he became something far greater than a British statesman, and took a place amid the greatest leaders of the human race. Amid the obstructions and the cynicism of a materialistic age he never lost his hold on the 'ideal'. And so it came to pass that wherever throughout the civilized world a race or nation of men were suffering from oppression, their thoughts turned toward Gladstone, and when that mighty voice was raised in their behalf Europe and the civilized world listened, and the breathing of new hopes entered into the hearts of men made desperate by long despair.

In the years that have gone by England has lost many men who served their country splendidly and round whose graves the British people deeply mourned; but round the deathbed of Gladstone the people of this island are joined in their sorrow by many peoples, and today throughout the Christian world – in many lands and in many tongues – prayers will be offered to that God on whom in his last supreme hour of trial Mr Gladstone humbly placed his firm reliance, begging that He will remember to His great servant how ardently he loved his fellow men, without distinction of race, while he lived among them, and how mightily he laboured for their good.

'*If they want war, then war they will have.*'

James Larkin
(1874–1947)

Speech before the tribunal of inquiry at Dublin Castle, 4 October 1913

'If they want war, then war they will have.'

On 26 August 1913, during Dublin's society event of the year – the Horse Show – 200 tram drivers and conductors alighted from their carriages mid-shift to protest at the dismissal of fellow workers. This began a dispute that would quickly turn into a pitched battle between workers and employers. It also established union leader James Larkin as the 'lion of the fold'.

Dublin in the early years of the 20th century had among the worst slums in western Europe. Formerly elegant Georgian terraces had become squalid and overcrowded tenements for the poor. Unemployment was endemic. Work for those lucky enough to have it was often sporadic, backbreaking and underpaid. Efforts to organize unskilled and casual workers into trade unions had led in 1908 to the formation of the Irish Transport and General Workers Union (ITGWU). Its leader, James 'Big Jim' Larkin, had been a docker in Liverpool and Belfast. He was a physically imposing man, with a combative personality and charisma to match. 'His genius is inflammatory,' said the *New Statesman* in September 1913, 'He preaches turmoil.'

Larkin's co-ordination of unskilled labour was stoutly resisted by most employers. These bosses, said the poet Yeats, were men obsessed by 'the greasy till'. One such individual was William Martin Murphy, among Ireland's foremost businessmen. His interests included the Dublin Tramway Company, the *Irish Independent*, the Imperial Hotel and Clery's department store. To foil Larkin's growing influence, Murphy sacked a large number of suspected trade unionists. Over the course of a week that summer, he laid off 40 workers at the *Independent*, 200 tramway men and 100 workers in the parcel room. It was this action that prompted strike action during the Horse Show.

The dispute quickly escalated. On 1 September, Jacob's biscuit factory locked out its workers. Other companies soon followed suit. By the end of the month, 25,000 workers had been turned away from work. Most were left in a state of destitution. One month into the lockout, the board of trade established a tribunal of inquiry. Larkin acted as counsel for the workers. This address on 4 October 1913 was a blazing indictment of Dublin employers. The inquiry found in favour of the workers, but employers refused to give way. The stalemate continued into the

BIOGRAPHY

Jim Larkin was born in Liverpool in 1874 to Irish parents. After moving to Belfast in 1907, he helped the following year to found the Irish Transport and General Workers' Union (ITGWU), an independent Irish union for unskilled labourers. After the 1913 lockout, Larkin moved to America, where he set up the Communist Party of the United States. Imprisoned for 'criminal anarchy' in 1920, he became something of a cause célèbre with visitors at Sing Sing Prison, including Charlie Chaplin. He was deported in 1923. His return to Dublin split the union movement that he had helped to found. Larkin nevertheless remained hugely popular with Dublin workers: thousands lined the route from Haddington Road church to Glasnevin Cemetery in 1947 to pay their last respects to 'Big Jim'.

New Year, before fizzling out in April 1914. The clash left the union crippled and Larkin exhausted. He left soon afterward for the United States, not to return for almost ten years, but with his status already assured as an icon of the left.

… I hope you will bear with me in putting before you as plainly as possible a reply somewhat of a personal character, but which I think will cover the matters dealt with during the last few days. The first point I want to make is that the employers in this city, and throughout Ireland generally, have put forward a claim that they have a right to deal with their own; that they have a right to use and exploit individuals as they please; that they have duties which they limit, and they have responsibilities which they also limit, in their operation. They take to themselves that they have all the rights that are given to men and to societies of men, but they deny the right of the men to claim that they also have a substantial claim on the share of the produce they produce, and they further say that they want no third party interference. They want to deal with their workingmen individually. They say that they are men of such paramount intelligence and so able in their organizing ability as captains of industry, who can always carry on their business in their own way, and they deny the right of the men and women who work for them to combine and try to assist one another in trying to improve their conditions of life …

'Go to the factories and see the maimed girls.'

What was the position of affairs in connection with life in industrial Ireland? Let them take the statement made by their own apologist … that there are 21,000 families – four and a half persons to a family – living in single rooms. Who are responsible? The gentlemen opposite would have to accept the responsibility. Of course they must. They said they control the means of life; then the responsibility rests upon them. Twenty-one thousand people multiplied by five, over 100,000 people huddled together in the putrid slums of Dublin, five in a room in cubic space less than 1000 feet, though the law lays it down that every human being should have 300 cubic feet.

We are determined that this shall no longer go on; we are determined the system shall stop; we are determined that Christ will not be crucified in Dublin by these men…

Let people who desire to know the truth go to the factories and see the maimed girls, the weak and sickly, whose eyes are being put out and their bodies scarred and their souls seared and when they were no longer able to be useful enough to gain their £1 a week, or whatever wage they earned, were thrown into the human scrap heap. These things were to be found in their midst, and yet the people who caused these conditions of wretchedness described workingmen as loafers …

'If they want war, then war they will have.'

I am concerned in something greater, something better, and something holier – a mutual relation between those carrying on industry in Ireland. These men (the employers) with their limited intelligence cannot see that. I cannot help that. I cannot compel them to look at the thing from my point of view. Surely they have a right to realize the work in which I am engaged. It is not to our interest to have men locked-out or on strike. We don't get double wages. They say 'Larkin is making £18 a week', and has made more than £18 a week, but he never got it unfortunately. I have lived among the working classes all my life. I have starved because men denied me food. I worked very hard at a very early age. I had no opportunities like the men opposite, but whatever opportunities I got I have availed of them. I am called anti-Christ and an atheist. If I were an atheist I would not deny it. I am a socialist and have always claimed to be a socialist.

'I will always be proud … in rescuing the workers of Dublin from the brutalizing and degrading conditions under which they laboured.'

I believe in a co-operative commonwealth. That is a long way ahead in Ireland. Why cannot I help as you can help in working the present system in a proper, reasonable way, conducive to both sides, and I have suggested the machinery that may be put into operation …

Can anyone say one word against me as a man? Can they make any disparagement of my character? Have I lessened the standard of life? Have I demoralized anyone? Is there anything in my private life or my public life of which I should feel ashamed? These men denounced me from the pulpit, and say I am making £18 a week and that I have a mansion in Dublin. The men who are described as Larkin's dupes are asked to go back. All this is done 2000 years after Christ appeared in Galilee. Why, these men are making people atheists – they are making them godless. But we are going to stop that.

When the position of the workers in Dublin was taken into consideration, was it any wonder that there was necessity for a Larkin to arise, and if there was one thing more than another in my life of which I will always be proud it was the part I have taken in rescuing the workers of Dublin from the brutalizing and degrading conditions under which they laboured.

We are out … to break down racial and sectarian barriers. My suggestion to the employers is that if they want peace we are prepared to meet them, but if they want war, then war they will have.

'*Ulster is asking to be let alone.*'

Edward Carson
(1854–1935)

Speech to the House of Commons, Westminster, 11 February 1914

'Ulster is asking to be let alone.'

The King's Speech delivered by George V to the Houses of Parliament on 10 February 1914 promised to be a momentous one for Ireland. Two years earlier the Commons had passed a home rule bill, but it had remained stuck in the (Conservative-dominated) House of Lords. Now the liberal government of Herbert Henry Asquith declared its intention to enact the bill. Among the first to condemn the move was the leader of the Unionist MPs in the House of Commons, Sir Edward Carson. Though melancholic and serious, Carson was a man possessed of 'a moral fervour almost fanatical in its intensity and an instinctive feel for high political drama' (Nicholas Mansergh). At no time was this flair for the dramatic married to high principle better displayed than in his response to the King's Speech on 11 February 1914.

Carson's speech was the elegant articulation of a complex worldview. Middle class, Dublin-born, Anglican and educated at Trinity College, Carson was typical of the Anglo-Irish tradition. When he was elected leader of Unionist MPs in 1910, he stood out (aside from the brilliance of his oratory) for not being from the northeast of the island nor of an Ulster Scots/Presbyterian background. This led to a divergence on partition. While many of his colleagues were happy to see Ireland divided if it saved them from home rule, Carson was determined to keep Ireland united within the Union. To this end, he saw the 'Ulster question' as a tactical device, believing that if he stopped home rule there, it would be a dead letter for the country as a whole.

Carson had been the first of almost half a million men and women to sign the

BIOGRAPHY

Edward Carson was born in 1854 in Harcourt Street, Dublin, to an 'Anglo-Irish' family. A brilliant barrister, he famously cross-examined Oscar Wilde in the Marquess of Queensbury's libel action in 1893. The previous year he had been elected as MP for Dublin University, becoming leader of the Unionist MPs from 1910 until 1921. He left the Commons to become a law lord in 1921. 'Loyalty is a strange thing,' Carson declared just days after Lloyd George had signed an Anglo-Irish Treaty with Sinn Féin, 'It is something you cannot get by sitting round a table and trying to find a formula for an Oath of Allegiance which means nothing. It is something born and bred in you.' He died in Kent in 1935 and was buried, after a state funeral, in St Anne's Cathedral, Belfast.

Ulster Solemn League and Covenant on 28 September 1912, and he subsequently helped to lead the Ulster Volunteer Force. He used the threat of civil war in Ireland to slow the progress of home rule. Only as its momentum continued after 1912 did he shift his objective from trying to secure unity to achieving the best deal for Ulster. Still, if the goal had changed, Carson's rhetoric had not. His contribution to the King's Speech debate made it clear that Ulster loyalists had no intention of being coerced into a devolved state with the rest of Ireland.

... What is the first lesson that we deduce or learn from this grave statement in His Majesty's speech? We have been two years discussing this question, and I certainly have been two years trying to make the position of the loyalists of Ireland known, and now, after two years, the first lesson we learn is this, that the bill of the government, on their own confession, has utterly failed to find a solution of the Irish question...

'Your only answer was ... to insult us.'

They are always talking of concessions to Ulster. Ulster is not asking for concessions. Ulster is asking to be let alone. When you talk of concessions, what you really mean is, 'We want to lay down what is the minimum of wrong we can do to Ulster.' Let me tell you that the results of two years' delay and the treatment we have received during these two years have made your task and made our task far more difficult. You have driven these men to enter into a covenant for their mutual protection. No doubt you have laughed at their covenant. Have a good laugh at it now. Well, so far as I am concerned, I am not the kind of man who will go over to Ulster one day and say, 'Enter into a covenant,' and go over the next day and say, 'Break it.' But there is something more. You have insulted them ...

Believe me, whatever way you settle the Irish question, there are only two ways to deal with Ulster. It is for statesmen to say which is the best and right one. She is not a part of the community which can be bought. She will not allow herself to be sold. You must therefore either coerce her if you go on, or you must, in the long run, by showing that good government can come under the home rule bill, try and win her over to the case of the rest of Ireland. You probably can coerce her – although I doubt it. If you do, what will be the disastrous consequences not only to Ulster, but to this country and the Empire? Will my fellow countryman, the leader of the Nationalist Party, have gained anything? I will agree with him – I do not believe he wants to triumph any more than I do. But will he have gained anything if he takes over these people and then applies for what he used to call – at all events his party used to call – the enemies of the people to come in and coerce them into obedience? No, sir, one false step taken in relation to Ulster will, in my opinion, render for ever impossible a solution of the Irish question. I say this to my nationalist fellow countrymen, and, indeed, also to the government: you have never tried to win over Ulster. You have never tried to understand her position. You have never alleged, and can never allege, that this bill gives her one atom of advantage. Nay, you cannot deny that it takes away many advantages that she has as a constituent part of the United Kingdom. You cannot deny that in the past she had produced the most loyal and law-abiding part of the citizens of Ireland. After all that, for these two years, every time we came before you your only answer to us – the majority of you, at all events – was to insult us, and to make little of us. I say to the leader of the Nationalist Party, if you want Ulster, go and take her, or go and win her...

'The interests of Ireland are at stake in this war.'

John Redmond
(1856–1918)

Speech at Woodenbridge, County Wicklow, 20 September 1914

Ireland by May 1914 was edging inch by slow inch towards home rule. The only question seemed to be whether there would be an exclusion scheme for Ulster. John Redmond, leader of the Irish Party, had endeavoured without success to broker an agreement with his unionist counterpart, Edward Carson. The Ulster Volunteer Force, numbering some 100,000 men, was threatening armed resistance. A conference at Buckingham Palace in July called by George V to establish a compromise between unionists and nationalists collapsed after three days. Civil war loomed.

The outbreak of war in Europe in August changed everything. Home rule was put on ice, as unionists and nationalists vied to see who could use the conflict for their own advantage. Edward Carson was first to promise that his (Ulster) Volunteers would act as defenders of Ireland against invasion. Redmond immediately pledged that his Volunteers would do the same. He was determined that Carson would not outflank him. The British government, he calculated, would repay this loyalty in the long run.

Redmond's backing of the British war effort won general support in Ireland. Even his unilateral promise of Volunteer support did not split that body. His decision the following month to urge the Volunteers to sign up to the British forces, first articulated in the Commons on 15 September and repeated five days later at a Volunteer meeting in Woodenbridge, County Wicklow, was more controversial. He meant it as a demonstration of Ireland's ability to organize an effective fighting force; others saw it as a betrayal of Irish nationality.

Eoin MacNeill disclaimed Redmond and took around 13,000 of the 188,000 members with him still under the name Irish Volunteers. Redmond's National Volunteers effectively collapsed afterwards. The Irish Volunteers went on to provide the cadre for the 1916 Easter Rising under the leadership of the IRB.

BIOGRAPHY

John Redmond was born in 1856 at Ballytrent, County Wexford, the eldest son of the local MP, William Redmond. He was educated at Clongowes Wood, County Kildare, and at Trinity College, Dublin. In 1876, he went to London as his father's assistant and became a clerk of the House of Commons. Elected as an MP in 1880, Redmond became leader of the anti-Parnellite faction following Parnell's death in 1891 and subsequently led the united party between 1900 and 1918. 'As a nationalist,' he said during the 1886 home rule debates, 'I do not regard as entirely palatable the idea that forever and a day Ireland's voice should be excluded from the councils of an empire which the genius and valour of her sons have done so much to build up and of which she is to remain.' Redmond was buried in 1918 in Wexford following a funeral mass at Westminster Cathedral.

'The interests of Ireland are at stake in this war.'

Fellow countrymen, it was fortunate chance that enabled me to be present here today. I was motoring past, and I did not know until I arrived here that this gathering of the Volunteers was to take place at Woodenbridge. I could not deny myself the pleasure and honour of waiting to meet you, to meet so many of those whom I have personally known for many long years, and to see them fulfilling a high duty to their country. I have no intention of making a speech. All I desire to say to you is that I congratulate you upon the favourable beginning of the work you have made.

You have only barely made a beginning. You will yet have hard work before you can call yourselves efficient soldiers, and you will have to have in your hand – every man – as efficient weapons as I am glad to see in hands of some, at any rate, of your numbers. Looking back as I naturally do, upon the history of Wicklow, I know that you will make efficient soldiers. Efficient soldiers for what?

'This war is undertaken in the defence of the highest principles of religion and morality.'

Wicklow Volunteers, in spite of the peaceful happiness and beauty of the scene in which we stand, remember this country at this moment is in a state of war, and your duty is a twofold duty. The duty of the manhood of Ireland is twofold. Its duty is, at all costs, to defend the shores of Ireland against foreign invasion. It is a duty more than that of taking care that Irish valour proves itself; on the field of war it has always proved itself in the past. The interests of Ireland – of the whole of Ireland – are at stake in this war. This war is undertaken in the defence of the highest principles of religion and morality and right, and it would be a disgrace for ever to our country and a reproach to her manhood and a denial of the lessons of her history if young Ireland confined their efforts to remaining at home to defend the shores of Ireland from an unlikely invasion, and to shrinking from the duty of proving on the field of battle that gallantry and courage which has distinguished our race all through its history. I say to you, therefore, your duty is twofold. I am glad to see such magnificent material for soldiers around me, and I say to you: go on drilling and make yourself efficient for the work, and then account yourselves as men, not only for Ireland itself, but wherever the fighting line extends, in defence of right, of freedom and religion in this war.

'The fools, the fools! They have left us our Fenian dead.'

Patrick Pearse
(1879–1916)

Address at O'Donovan Rossa's funeral, Glasnevin Cemetery, Dublin, 1 August 1915

*'The fools, the fools! They have left us
our Fenian dead.'*

Jeremiah O'Donovan Rossa was a founder-member of the Irish Republican Brotherhood (IRB). He spent a number of periods in prison, and was sentenced to 20 years in 1865. During that time he was elected as a Member of Parliament for Tipperary, even though as a convicted felon he would have been disbarred from taking his seat. Eventually, in 1871, O'Donovan Rossa was offered early release on the condition that he left the country. He travelled to New York, but remained an active Fenian in exile, orchestrating a bombing campaign in Britain and writing a series of popular accounts of his time in prison.

When O'Donovan Rossa died in 1915, IRB leaders were quick to see the propaganda potential in bringing him home. Thomas Clarke sent word to New York that the body should come home immediately. With plans for a rising already underway, the Volunteers had been keeping a low profile to avoid arrests. Yet for the old Fenian's funeral, Clarke and his comrades decided that the occasion should be spectacular, with large numbers of Volunteers present and as much fiery oratory as could be mustered. To that end, Clarke chose Patrick Pearse, a senior member of the Volunteers and the IRB, to give the oration. Pearse had impressed Clarke two years earlier with his address at a Tone commemoration in Bodenstown. Then he had proclaimed to the Volunteers that they stood at the 'holiest place in Ireland; holier to us even than the place where Patrick sleeps in Down. Patrick brought us life, but this man died for us.' Now at O'Donovan Rossa's graveside in Glasnevin, Pearse surpassed himself.

The funeral attracted a great deal of press coverage, and settled the question of the rival claims on Rossa – and by extension the Fenians more generally – firmly with Pearse and his comrades. As the first major public event to be staged by the Volunteers it was a remarkable success. Pearse's address – described as a 'masterpiece of patriotic rhetoric' – was widely noted and reprinted. It sounded, as one contemporary later put it, the Reveille of Easter: the next notable oration by Pearse would be given in 1916 from the steps of the GPO as commandant-general and president of the Provisional Republic.

> **BIOGRAPHY**
>
> **Patrick Pearse** was born in 1879 at Great Brunswick (later Pearse) Street in Dublin, the son of an English father and an Irish mother. He was educated by the Christian Brothers and at the Jesuit-run University College Dublin. Active in the Gaelic League from 1895, he came to prominence as editor of its newspaper, *Claidhemah Soluis*. In 1913 he joined the Volunteers and the Irish Republican Brotherhood (which co-opted him onto its supreme council). Following the Easter Rising, Pearse was executed by firing squad on 4 May in Kilmainham Prison. His brother Willie was executed on the same day. They were both buried in Arbour Hill.

It has seemed right, before we turn away from this place in which we have hid the mortal remains of O'Donovan Rossa, that one among us should, in the name of all, speak the praise of that valiant man, and endeavour to formulate the thought and the hope that are in us as we stand around his grave. And if there is anything that makes it fitting that I, rather than some other, I rather than one of the grey-haired men who were young with him and shared in his labour and in his suffering, should speak here, it is perhaps that I may be taken as speaking on behalf of a new generation that has been rebaptized in the Fenian faith, and that has accepted the responsibility of carrying out the Fenian programme. I propose to you then that, here by the grave of this unrepentant Fenian, we renew our baptismal vows; that, here by the grave of this unconquered and unconquerable man, we ask of God, each one for himself, such unshakeable purpose, such high and gallant courage, such unbreakable strength of soul as belonged to O'Donovan Rossa.

Deliberately here we avow ourselves, as he avowed himself in the dock, Irishmen of one allegiance only. We of the Irish Volunteers, and you others who are associated with us in today's task and duty, are bound together and must stand together henceforth in brotherly union for the achievement of the freedom of Ireland. And we know only one definition of freedom: it is Tone's definition, it is Mitchel's definition, it is Rossa's definition. Let no man blaspheme the cause that the dead generations of Ireland served by giving it any other name and definition than their name and their definition.

'Not free merely, but Gaelic as well; not Gaelic merely, but free as well.'

We stand at Rossa's grave not in sadness but rather in exaltation of spirit that it has been given to us to come thus into so close a communion with that brave and splendid Gael. Splendid and holy causes are served by men who are themselves splendid and holy. O'Donovan Rossa was splendid in the proud manhood of him, splendid in the heroic grace of him, splendid in the Gaelic strength and clarity and truth of him. And all that splendour and pride and strength was compatible with a humility and a simplicity of devotion to Ireland, to all that was olden and beautiful and Gaelic in Ireland, the holiness and simplicity of patriotism of a Michael O'Clery or of an Eoghan O'Growney. The clear true eyes of this man almost alone in his day visioned Ireland as we of today would surely have her: not free merely, but Gaelic as well; not Gaelic merely, but free as well.

In a closer spiritual communion with him now than ever before or perhaps ever again, in a spiritual communion with those of his day, living and dead, who suffered with him in English prisons, in communion of spirit too with our own dear

*'The fools, the fools! They have left us
our Fenian dead.'*

comrades who suffer in English prisons today, and speaking on their behalf as well as our own, we pledge to Ireland our love, and we pledge to English rule in Ireland our hate. This is a place of peace, sacred to the dead, where men should speak with all charity and with all restraint; but I hold it a Christian thing, as O'Donovan Rossa held it, to hate evil, to hate untruth, to hate oppression, and, hating them, to strive to overthrow them.

'Life springs from death; and from the graves of patriot men and women spring living nations.'

Our foes are strong and wise and wary but, strong and wise and wary as they are, they cannot undo the miracles of God who ripens in the hearts of young men the seeds sown by the young men of a former generation. And the seeds sown by the young men of '65 and '67 are coming to their miraculous ripening today. Rulers and defenders of realms had need to be wary if they would guard against such processes. Life springs from death; and from the graves of patriot men and women spring living nations. The defenders of this realm have worked well in secret and in the open. They think that they have pacified Ireland. They think that they have purchased half of us and intimidated the other half. They think that they have foreseen everything, think that they have provided against everything; but the fools, the fools, the fools! – they have left us our Fenian dead, and while Ireland holds these graves, Ireland unfree shall never be at peace.

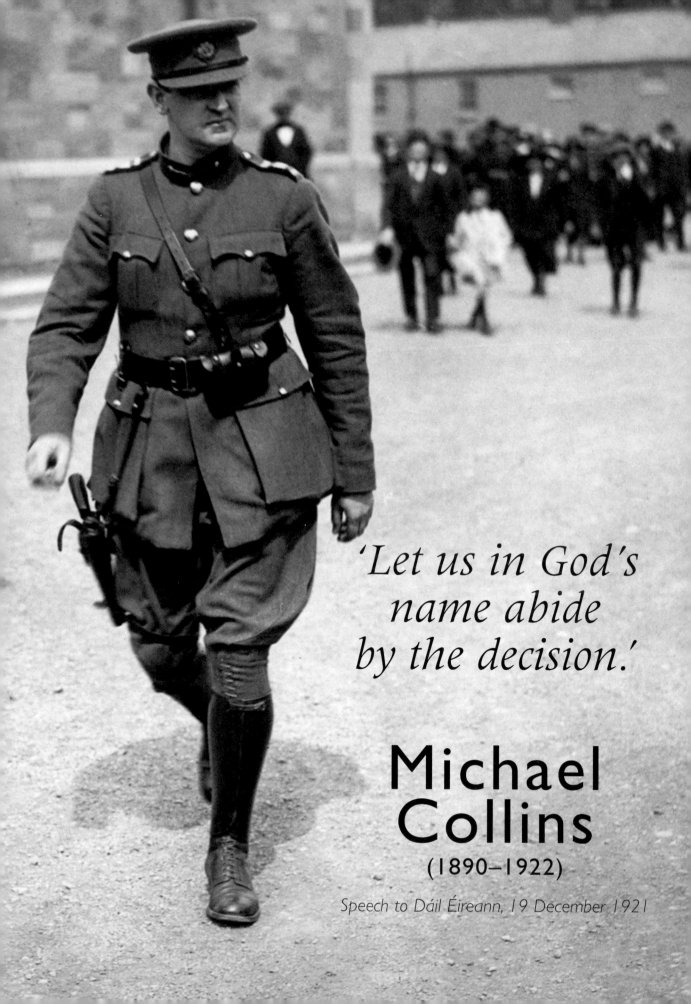

'Let us in God's name abide by the decision.'

Michael Collins

(1890–1922)

Speech to Dáil Éireann, 19 December 1921

'Let us in God's name abide by the decision.'

On 6 December 1921 representatives of the British and Dáil governments signed the articles of agreement of the Anglo-Irish Treaty. This provided for the establishment of an Irish Free State that would be a dominion of the British Empire. British armed forces would maintain a presence in the country, but only through the retention of strategic ports. Six counties would be partitioned from the new state. A boundary commission would meet to establish the border.

When the Irish negotiating team returned home, Éamon de Valera – who had declined to go to London – eviscerated them for the agreement itself and for signing without first consulting him. Yet when Cabinet came to vote on the Treaty, it was passed, albeit by a single vote. The next step was ratification by Dáil Éireann. This began an intense, often high-minded, occasionally vitriolic battle not just for the hearts and minds of the deputies, but for those of the people. Men and women who had fought together now found themselves on opposing sides of the argument. The debates represent probably the most crucial, heart-wrenching exchanges in modern Irish politics. They took place in University College Dublin, at Earlsfort Terrace, beginning on 14 December and lasting 15 days (with a short break for Christmas).

Early sessions in the debate were held in private, but later ones took place in public and were well documented in the press. They were dominated by the senior figures in the Republican movement, and in particular by Éamon de Valera, who spoke frequently and made numerous emotional interjections. Yet the debates saw him oddly below par, perhaps because he spoke so often and failed to refine his thinking into one searing contribution. Michael Collins, on the other hand, was at his charismatic best. Although much of what he said was not new, this speech on 19 December distilled the case for the Treaty into one powerful and eloquent message. Even Erskine Childers, who spoke immediately after Collins to refute his arguments, expressed his admiration for a 'manly, eloquent, and worthy speech'. Collins's biographer, Peter Hart, concludes that it was 'easily the best speech of Collins's life and one of the greatest statements of political rationality in Irish history'.

Dáil Éireann passed the Treaty by seven votes on 7 January 1922.

BIOGRAPHY

Michael Collins was born in 1890 in Clonakilty, County Cork, and emigrated at the age of 15 to London, where he joined the Irish Republican Brotherhood (IRB). He travelled back to Dublin for the Easter Rising and afterwards was interned in Wales. He was a prominent Sinn Féin and Volunteer activist, as well as president of the IRB, and played a pivotal role in military strategy during the war of independence. A signatory of the 1921 Anglo-Irish Treaty, he became chairman of the provisional government in January 1922 and commander-in-chief of the national army. Collins was fatally wounded during an ambush at Béal na Bláth in West Cork on 22 August 1922. His funeral was an occasion of mass grief. He is buried in Glasnevin Cemetery.

Much has been said in Private Session about the action of the plenipotentiaries in signing at all or in signing without first putting their document before the Cabinet … Now, I want to make this clear. The answer which I gave and that signature which I put on that document would be the same in Dublin or in Berlin, or in New York or in Paris. If we had been in Dublin the difference in distance would have made this difference, that we would have been able to consult not only the members of the Cabinet but many members of the Dáil and many good friends. There has been talk about 'the atmosphere of London' and there has been talk about 'slippery slopes'. Such talk is beside the point. I knew the atmosphere of London of old and I knew many other things about it of old. If the members knew so much about 'slippery slopes' before we went there why did they not speak then? The slopes were surely slippery, but it is easy to be wise afterwards. I submit that such observations are entirely beside the point. And if my signature has been given in error, I stand by it whether it has or not, and I am not going to take refuge behind any kind of subterfuge. I stand up over that signature and I give the same decision at this moment in this assembly.

'I did not break down before that bluff.'

It has also been suggested that the delegation broke down before the first bit of English bluff. I would remind the deputy who used that expression that England put up quite a good bluff for the last five years here and I did not break down before that bluff. And does anybody think that the respect I compelled from them in a few years was in any way lowered during two months of negotiations? That also is beside the point.

The results of our labour are before the Dáil. Reject or accept.

The President has suggested that a greater result could have been obtained by more skilful handling. Perhaps so. But there again the fault is not the delegation's; it rests with the Dáil. It is not afterwards the Dáil should have found out our limitations. Surely the Dáil knew it when they selected us, and our abilities could not have been expected to increase because we were chosen as plenipotentiaries by the Dáil.

The delegates have been blamed for various things. It is scarcely too much to say that they have been blamed for not returning with recognition of the Irish Republic. They are blamed, at any rate, for not having done much better … It is further suggested that by the result of their labours the delegation made a resumption of hostilities certain. That again rests with the Dáil; they should have chosen a better delegation, and it was before we went to London that should have been done, not when we returned …

'Let us in God's name abide by the decision.'

'Send us a thousand men fully equipped.'

I say that this Treaty gives us, not recognition of the Irish Republic, but it gives us more recognition on the part of Great Britain and the associated States than we have got from any other nation. Again I want to speak plainly. America did not recognize the Irish Republic. As things in London were coming to a close I received cablegrams from America. I understand that my name is pretty well known in America, and what I am going to say now will make me unpopular there for the rest of my life, but I am not going to say anything or hide anything for the sake of American popularity. I received a cablegram from San Francisco, saying, 'Stand fast, we will send you a million dollars a month.' Well, my reply to that is, 'Send us half-a-million and send us a thousand men fully equipped.'

I received another cablegram from a branch of the American Association for the Recognition of the Irish Republic and they said to me, 'Don't weaken now, stand with de Valera.' Well, let that branch come over and stand with us both.

'I want to say that there was never an Irishman placed in such a position as I was by reason of these negotiations.'

The question before me was, were we going to go on with this fight, without referring it to the Irish people, for the sake of propaganda in America? I was not going to take that responsibility.

And as this may be the last opportunity I shall ever have of speaking publicly to the Dáil, I want to say that there was never an Irishman placed in such a position as I was by reason of these negotiations. I had got a certain name, whether I deserved it or not, and I knew when I was going over there that I was being placed in a position that I could not reconcile, and that I could not in the public mind be reconciled with what they thought I stood for, no matter what we brought back – and if we brought back the recognition of the Republic – but I knew that the English would make a greater effort if I were there than they would if I were not there, and I didn't care if my popularity was sacrificed or not. I should have been unfair to my own country if I did not go there. Members of the Dáil well remember that I protested against being selected …

'I stand for every action, no matter how it looked.'

I only want to say that I stand for every action as an individual member of the Cabinet, which I suppose I shall be no longer; I stand for every action, no matter how it looked publicly, and I shall always like the men to remember me like that. In coming to the decision I did I tried to weigh what my own responsibility was.

Deputies have spoken about whether dead men would approve of it, and they have spoken of whether children yet unborn will approve of it, but few of them have spoken as to whether the living approve of it. In my own small way I tried to have before my mind what the whole lot of them would think of it. And the proper way for us to look at it is in that way.

'Let us take that responsibility ourselves and let us in God's name abide by the decision.'

There is no man here who has more regard for the dead men than I have. I don't think it is fair to be quoting them against us. I think the decision ought to be a clear decision on the documents as they are before us – on the Treaty as it is before us. On that we shall be judged, as to whether we have done the right thing in our own conscience or not.

Don't let us put the responsibility, the individual responsibility, upon anybody else. Let us take that responsibility ourselves and let us in God's name abide by the decision.

Mary MacSwiney (right) with activist Maud Gonne MacBride and writer Miss Barry Delaney outside Mountjoy prison during the hungerstrike

'The grossest act of betrayal.'

Mary MacSwiney
(1872–1942)

Speech to Dáil Éireann, 7 January 1922

The Treaty debates had seen some reasoned argument and a lot of invective. The numbers for (64) and against (57) had been very close, and over the weeks some deputies had changed their minds. Several might have swung behind the Treaty after a Christmas at home, where they had the opportunity to gauge the views of their constituents, who tended to support the settlement. One who stuck steadfastly to her original position, however, was Mary MacSwiney. A self-professed 'doctrinaire republican', MacSwiney was president of Cumann na mBan, the women's auxiliary of the Irish Republican Army (IRA), and the older sister of Terence MacSwiney, the republican lord mayor of Cork who had died on hunger strike in Brixton Prison in 1920. MacSwiney was the embodiment of a die-hard, unafraid to show her contempt for the pro-Treatyites.

When the result in favour of the Treaty was announced on 7 January 1922, there was a terrible foreboding in the chamber. Collins and de Valera were visibly upset at the fissure that had developed in the movement. Each feared what might follow and made some attempt at immediate reconciliation. De Valera had declared that he would facilitate a hand-over to a new president. Collins remarked that he had always tried to do his best for de Valera, who had 'exactly the same position in [my] heart now as he always had'.

Mary MacSwiney, however, was not taken by the anguished mood. Like Mrs Pearse (mother of Patrick and Willie) and Kathleen Clarke (widow of the IRB leader Thomas), MacSwiney had been elected to the Dáil on the record of a deceased relative. Each retained a strong conviction that the Treaty was a sell-out that dishonoured the memories of their departed loved ones. Enraged by the result of the vote and the subsequent language of reconciliation, MacSwiney launched into this vicious tirade. Her attack was effectively the last word in the Dáil's Treaty debate.

BIOGRAPHY

Mary MacSwiney was born in London in 1872 to Irish parents, who brought the family back to Cork when she was six. She was educated at Queen's College, Cork, and at Cambridge, where she qualified as a teacher. Arrested at the school where she was teaching in 1916 on suspicion of involvement in the Easter Rising, MacSwiney lost her job and so founded her own school, St Ita's. She campaigned for her younger brother, Terence, during the 1918 election and was later active in bringing his death by hunger strike to widescale public attention. Elected to the Dáil in 1921 as one of the foremost opponents of the Anglo-Irish Treaty, she held her seat until 1927. Mary MacSwiney died in Cork in 1942 and was buried in St Joseph's Cemetery.

'The grossest act of betrayal.'

I claim my right, before matters go any further, to register my protest, because I look upon this act tonight worse than I look upon the Act of Castlereagh. I, for one, will have neither hand, act nor part in helping the Irish Free State to carry this nation of ours, this glorious nation that has been betrayed here tonight, into the British Empire – either with or without your hands up.

I maintain here now that this is the grossest act of betrayal that Ireland ever endured. I know some of you have done it from good motives; soldiers have done it to get a gun, God help them! Others, because they thought it best in some other way. I do not want to say a word that would prevent them from coming back to their Mother Republic; but I register my protest, and not one bit of help that we can give will we give them. The speech we have heard sounded very beautiful – as the late minister of finance can do it; he has played up to the gallery in this thing, but I tell you it may sound very beautiful but it will not do. Ireland stands on her republican government and that republican government cannot touch the pitch of the Free State without being fouled; and here and now I call on all true republicans; we all want to protect the public safety; it is our side that will do its best to protect the public safety. We want no such terrible troubles in the country as faction fights; we can never descend to the faction fights of former days; we have established a government, and we will have to protect it.

'There can be no union between the representatives of the Irish Republic and the so-called Free State.'

Therefore, let there be no misunderstanding, no soft talk, no *ráiméis* ['nonsense'] at this last moment of the betrayal of our country; no soft talk about union; you cannot unite a spiritual Irish Republic and a betrayal worse than Castlereagh's, because it was done for the Irish nation. You may talk about the will of the Irish people, as Arthur Griffith did; you know it is not the will of the Irish people; it is the fear of the Irish people, as the lord mayor of Cork says; and tomorrow or another day when they come to their senses, they will talk of those who betrayed them today as they talk of Castlereagh. Make no doubt about it. This is a betrayal, a gross betrayal; and the fact is that it is only a small majority, and that majority is not united; half of them look for a gun and the other half are looking for the fleshpots of the Empire. I tell you here there can be no union between the representatives of the Irish Republic and the so-called Free State.

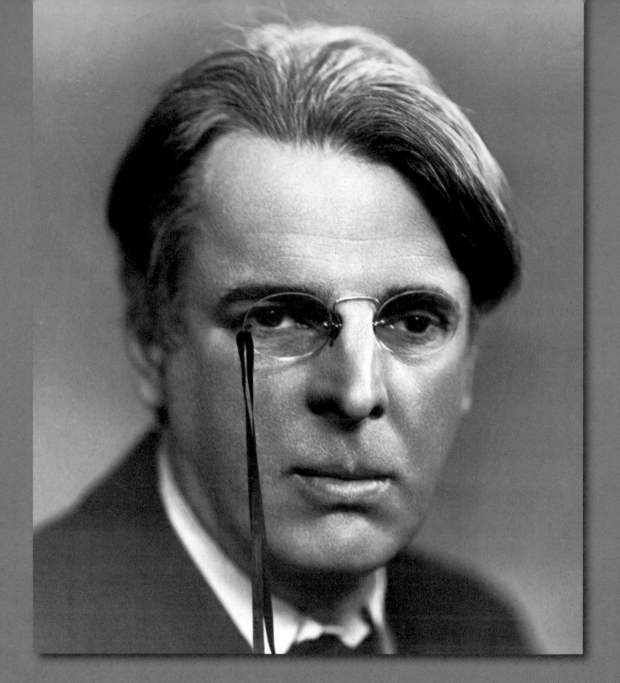

'We are no petty people.'

William Butler Yeats

(1865–1939)

Speech to Seanad Éireann, 11 June 1925

The 1922 Irish Free State constitution contained provisions on religious liberty and established a bicameral legislature that offered Protestants the possibility of representation in the upper house far exceeding their numbers. A senator who held his seat thanks in some part to his status as a Protestant was the poet W.B. Yeats.

This constitutional provision was the subject of regular debate. For the Catholic hierarchy, many of the Catholic laity and a significant number of politicians, Irish independence had not been won to establish a non-sectarian liberal democracy. The church consistently agitated for legislation in line with its moral and social teaching, including on issues of censorship and restrictions on intoxicating liquor. In the pious and austere government of Cumann na nGaedheal, the church found a partner happy to oblige.

Nothing vexed the church more than the issue of divorce, which was notionally available through the Senate. The Irish attorney-general suggested that the government ought to clarify 'provision for divorce bills for those who approve of that sort of thing' (i.e. Protestants). W.T. Cosgrave, the head of government, flatly rejected that advice. He had been advised by the church that every baptized person, whether Catholic or not, was subject to canon law. In the eyes of the Catholic hierarchy, it was impossible for the state to distinguish between Catholics and Protestants in the matter of divorce. 'The church was the mentor,' writes historian Patrick Murray, 'and Cosgrave the willing pupil.'

Although many Protestants personally opposed divorce, the government's decision to ban it was seen as a sectarian act. This was a direct attack on the Protestant liberal ethos, which regarded such issues as matters for the individual conscience. It was in this context that W.B. Yeats made a furious attack on the government and the Catholic church from the floor of the Senate in 1925. His aloof, patrician manner was ideally suited to an excoriating judgment delivered from on high, and to making an Olympian defence of Protestant achievement in advancing Ireland's cause. The speech, with its reference to 'the people of Swift ... the people of Emmet', self-consciously echoed Grattan's words 'Spirit of Swift! Spirit of Molyneux!'

BIOGRAPHY

W.B. Yeats was born in Sandymount, Dublin, in 1865 and moved at the age of two to London, where his father, John Butler Yeats, established himself as a noted portrait painter. Educated at the Godolphin School and then the Metropolitan School of Art in Dublin, Yeats became the leading poet of the Anglo-Irish literary revival and co-founded the Abbey Theatre in 1904. W.T. Cosgrave appointed him a senator in December 1922. He won the Nobel Prize for literature the following year. Yeats left Ireland for the French Riviera in 1938 due to failing health and died at Roquebrune early the next year. He was reinterred in 1948 in Drumcliff, County Sligo.

I speak on this question after long hesitation and with a good deal of anxiety, but it is sometimes one's duty to come down to absolute fundamentals for the sake of the education of the people. I have no doubt whatever that there will be no divorce in this country for some time. I do not expect to influence a vote in this House. I am not speaking to this House. It is the custom of those who do address the House to speak sometimes to the reporters.

(AN CATHAOIRLEACH: Perhaps the senator would please address me. I do not think that Senator Yeats intended to be uncomplimentary to the House, but his observation looked like it.)

I did not intend to be uncomplimentary. I should have said I do not intend to speak merely to the House. I have no doubt whatever, if circumstances were a little different, a very easy solution would be found for this whole difficulty. I judge from conversations that I have had with various persons that many would welcome a very simple solution, namely, that the Catholic members should remain absent when a Bill of Divorce was brought before the House that concerned Protestants and non-Catholics only, and that it would be left to the Protestant members, or some committee appointed by those Protestant members, to be dealt with. I think it would be the first instinct of the members of both Houses to adopt some such solution and it is obvious, I think, that from every point of view of national policy and national reputation that would be a wise policy.

'You will put a wedge into the midst of this nation.'

It is perhaps the deepest political passion with this nation that North and South be united into one nation. If it ever comes that North and South unite, the North will not give up any liberty which she already possesses under her constitution. You will then have to grant to another people what you refuse to grant to those within your borders. If you show that this country, Southern Ireland, is going to be governed by Catholic ideas and by Catholic ideas alone, you will never get the North. You will create an impassable barrier between South and North, and you will pass more and more Catholic laws, while the North will, gradually, assimilate its divorce and other laws to those of England. You will put a wedge into the midst of this nation. I do not think this House has ever made a more serious decision than the decision which, I believe, it is about to make on this question. You will not get the North if you impose on the minority what the minority consider to be oppressive legislation. I have no doubt whatever that in the next few years the minority will make it perfectly plain that it does consider it exceedingly oppressive legislation to deprive it of rights which it has held since the 17th century. These rights were won by the labours of John Milton and other great men, and won after strife, which is a famous part of the history of the Protestant people.

There is a reason why this country did not act upon what was its first impulse, and why this House and the Dáil did not act on their first impulse. Some of you may probably know that when the committee was set up to draw up the constitution of the Free State, it was urged to incorporate in the constitution the indissolubility of marriage and refused to do so. That was the expression of the political mind of Ireland. You are now urged to act on the advice of men who do not express the political mind, but who express the religious mind. I admit it must be exceedingly difficult for members of this House to resist the pressure that has been brought upon them. In the long warfare of this country with England the Catholic clergy took the side of the people, and owing to that they possess here an influence that they do not possess anywhere else in Europe…

'You are to force your theology upon persons who are not of your religion.'

I am sure it is difficult for members of this House to resist the advice of Archbishop O'Donnell. Addressing the Catholic Truth Society in October last he used these words:

'No power on earth can break the marriage bond until death … that is true of all baptized persons no matter what the denomination may be. To be sure we hear that a section of our fellow countrymen favour divorces. Well, with nothing but respect and sympathy for all our neighbours, we have to say that we place the marriages of such people higher than they do themselves. Their marriages are unbreakable before God and we cannot disobey God by helping to break them.'

'It is not a question of finding it legally difficult or impossible to grant to a minority what the majority does not wish for itself.'

That is to say, you are to legislate on purely theological grounds and you are to force your theology upon persons who are not of your religion. It is not a question of finding it legally difficult or impossible to grant to a minority what the majority does not wish for itself. You are to insist upon members of the Church of Ireland or members of no church taking a certain view of biblical criticism, or of the authority of the text upon which that criticism is exercised, a view that they notoriously do not take. If you legislate upon such grounds there is no reason why you should stop there. There is no reason why you should not forbid civil marriages altogether seeing that civil marriage is not marriage in the eyes of the church… [*following a complaint by another senator that his reading of the speech was out of order, Yeats continued*] These are topics on which it is desirable that the use of words should be carefully weighed beforehand. That must be my excuse. It is just as much adultery according to that view as the remarriage of divorced persons is. Nor do I see why you should stop at that, for we teach in our schools and universities and print in our books many things which the Catholic church does not approve of. Once you attempt legislation upon religious grounds you open the way for every kind of intolerance and for every kind of religious persecution …

'We are the people of Burke; we are the people of Grattan.'

I think it is tragic that within three years of this country gaining its independence we should be discussing a measure which a minority of this nation considers to be grossly oppressive. I am proud to consider myself a typical man of that minority. We against whom you have done this thing, are no petty people. We are one of the great stocks of Europe. We are the people of Burke; we are the people of Grattan; we are the people of Swift, the people of Emmet, the people of Parnell. We have created the most of the modern literature of this country. We have created the best of its political intelligence. Yet I do not altogether regret what has happened. I shall be able to find out, if not I, my children will be able to find out whether we have lost our stamina or not. You have defined our position and have given us a popular following. If we have not lost our stamina then your victory will be brief, and your defeat final, and when it comes this nation may be transformed.

'*The Blueshirts will be victorious in the Irish Free State.*'

John A. Costello
(1891–1976)

Speech to Dáil Éireann, 28 February 1934

On 16 February 1932, voters went to the polls in one of the most important general elections in the history of the Free State. The result – victory for Éamon de Valera and Fianna Fáil – ended ten years of Cumann na nGaedheal government. The election of a party rooted in the anti-Treaty tradition was a momentous step in normalizing party politics after the civil war. Yet mistrust died hard. There were rumours that Fianna Fáil's opponents were organizing a putsch. On the first day of the new Dáil, many deputies were rumoured to have arrived at Leinster House equipped with revolvers, just in case. The change of government passed off peacefully in the end, but strong resentment toward the new administration remained.

The Army Comrades Association (ACA) provided a rallying point for this discontent. The ACA had been highly effective in protecting Cumann na nGaedheal speakers against paramilitary violence. '[This] ensured the relatively peaceful organization of elections and political activity,' writes Brian Girvin, ' … at a time when some openly denied Cumann na nGaedheal's right to free speech.' When de Valera won another election in 1933, some of the government's enemies, including elements within the ACA, began asking whether a democratic system that could deliver Fianna Fáil to power might be fatally flawed.

By April 1933, the ACA, led by the former police commissioner Eoin O'Duffy, had been transformed into the National Guard. It adopted a uniform that included a distinctive blue shirt. The organization styled itself as an Irish, Christian organization (no foreigners, no Jews) that opposed political parties and in which trade unions would be banned. Notwithstanding the earlier efforts of the ACA in promoting democracy, the appearance of the blueshirt uniform, fascist-style salutes and an anti-democratic programme just months after Hitler and the Brownshirts had taken power in Berlin caused widespread consternation across the Irish political spectrum.

De Valera reacted decisively by banning the National Guard. It responded in September 1933 by combining with Cumann na nGaedheal and the small Centre Party to form Fine Gael under the leadership of O'Duffy. Many

BIOGRAPHY

John A. Costello was born at an address on the North Circular Road in Dublin in 1891. Called to the Bar in 1914, he joined the staff of the attorney-general in 1922 and subsequently held that office between 1926 and 1932 during the Cosgrave administrations. In 1948 he was invited to lead the first inter-party government when it became clear that coalition partners would not serve under the Fine Gael leader, General Richard Mulcahy. After heading the government in 1948–51 and 1954–7, he returned to the backbenches in 1959. He continued to practise until a short time before his death in Dublin in 1976. His son Declan also served as attorney-general (1973–7) and subsequently was appointed a judge of the High Court.

Opposition deputies defiantly continued to wear the blueshirt livery in the Oireachtas. Thus de Valera moved to crush the movement by stripping members of their most potent symbol. In February 1934 he introduced a bill to prohibit the wearing of uniforms in public. Similar measures were in force in most European countries that had not yet succumbed to fascism. In Britain the Home Office was considering legislation to deal with the Blackshirts.

Prominent among those who opposed the Wearing of Uniform (Restriction) Bill was John A. Costello, the future Fine Gael taoiseach. 'The Blackshirts were victorious in Italy and the Hitler Shirts were victorious in Germany,' he declared in this speech of 28 February 1934, 'as, assuredly, in spite of this bill and in spite of the Public Safety Act, the Blueshirts will be victorious in the Irish Free State.'

... There are so many reasons why deputies should vote against this bill, why every possible effort should be made to prevent it ever becoming law, that it is difficult to choose between them. I propose to take two main reasons. In the first place, this is a bill, as the minister for justice has frankly admitted – perhaps not in so many words – brought in by a political party which, for the moment forms the government, against a political party which, for the moment forms the chief opposition in this State and in this House. It is brought in against this political party by another political party, to be operated, if it ever becomes law, by a political police force. That is my first objection to this bill. My second objection is, if possible, perhaps a more fundamental objection, because it is a bill which is an invasion of individual rights and of the constitutional freedom which was guaranteed to the citizens of this state by the constitution which was brought into force on 6 December 1922. Deputies should pause before they give any support to the precedent that is set up by this bill. As I submit to the House and will show, it is an effort to prevent a lawful political movement, merely because that lawful political movement, as I mentioned on a previous occasion, menaces the political longevity of the Fianna Fáil Party ...

'That is the real danger.'

It is only one step from preventing a political party pursuing its ideas and aims by particular methods which are anti-phatic to the political party at the moment in power; to preventing a political party from functioning in a lawful way in this State merely because it is thought to be a menace to the political longevity of the political party in power. That is the real danger that lies in this bill. Even if the ministry were honest – I say and believe that they are not honest and their actions over the last 12 months have proved how dishonest they are – this is not a bill that ought to be passed by this House. No matter what they may think, the present government will not be there for all time so that another government with this precedent in front of them – with the same ridiculous reasons that the minister for justice gave today to bolster up this measure – may use similar provisions for the purpose of stifling lawful political activity, the lawful expression of political activity in this country which was politically uneducated in 1922, which is still, in some measure, politically uneducated and can only be politically educated along proper lines by the normal development of political parties and the clash of political ideas. This bill is going to put an end to that. It is going to set a precedent for anybody who wishes to stifle for all time such portions of the right of freedom of speech and the right of free association as will be left to the citizen of this State when the present government have been put out of power…

We wear a blue shirt, or those of us who happen to be members of the League of Youth, wear a blue shirt, and the girls wear blue blouses, not for the purpose of creating disorder, as the minister for justice would have us believe, but for the purpose of showing their comradeship and to indicate the decent people who are present at meetings and not the rowdies who are really the cause of disturbance at public meetings. The wearing of a uniform, so far from being provocative or unlawful, is adopted by our people so that we will be able to know that we have decent people, and so that, when there are disturbances in the crowd, the people who are creating the disturbance may be distinctly seen, and no one can say that it is the Blueshirts that are causing the disturbances at meetings.

'The Blackshirts were victorious in Italy … the Hitler Shirts were victorious in Germany.'

The minister gave extracts from various laws on the continent, but he carefully refrained from drawing attention to the fact that the Blackshirts were victorious in Italy and that the Hitler Shirts were victorious in Germany, as, assuredly, in spite of this bill and in spite of the Public Safety Act, the Blueshirts will be victorious in the Irish Free State … The minister bans political emblems of all kinds, classes and descriptions. Every article, every token, every emblem of any kind that may be regarded as indicating support of a particular political party is unlawful. I want to repeat here what I said in another place recently – and it is relevant to the charge that I have made that the present government, so far from upholding the law and bringing it into repute, is bringing it into disrepute – that it is a bad thing, as one writer on the relations between criminal law and morality has recently stated, that crimes should go unpunished; but it is worse that that which the general sense of the community regards as no crime should be made by law into a crime. That is what is being done by this bill. New crimes are being created which no single individual, beyond the front bench of the Fianna Fáil Party, believes are crimes. The general sense of the community is being revolted by this, and it will tend to bring the law into disrepute instead of respect…

'We are a Protestant Parliament and a Protestant State.'

Sir James Craig

(1871–1940)

Speech to the House of Commons of Northern Ireland, Stormont, 24 April 1934

During celebrations for 12 July in 1932, the Northern Ireland prime minister, James Craig, had remarked that 'ours is a Protestant government and I am an Orangeman.' He soon developed this further by saying he was an Orangeman first and a politician second. Then, famously, he declared in 1933 that he stood for a 'Protestant Parliament and a Protestant State' (often misquoted as a 'Protestant Parliament for a Protestant People').

Craig later argued that he was not being aggressively sectarian, but was simply mirroring the contemporary rhetoric of the Free State. Éamon de Valera, after all, had described himself as a Catholic first, Ireland as 'a Catholic nation', and had once reminded the papal legate of the words of St Patrick that, 'even as you are children of Christ, be you also children of Rome.'

The historian George Boyce has even suggested of Craig that not only his words but his 'whole career can be regarded as reactive, fashioned in opposition to the claims of Irish nationalism'.

Critics of Craig pointed out that while de Valera's words were celebrations of his own complex identity and the faith of the vast majority of the population of the Irish Free State, Craig's were uttered in the context of his support for a discriminatory regime.

Either way, few doubted that in declaring a fierce pride in a Protestant state, he spoke for the majority in Northern Ireland.

BIOGRAPHY

Sir James Craig was born in Belfast in 1871, the son of a whiskey-distilling millionaire (after whom he was named). Educated at Merchiston Castle School in Edinburgh, he returned to Belfast in 1892 to found a stockbroking firm before joining the Royal Irish Rifles in 1900. He fought in South Africa, where he was briefly taken prisoner. Elected Unionist MP for East Down in 1906, Craig remained at Westminster until 1921. He became prime minister of Northern Ireland in 1921 and served until his sudden death at home in Glencraig, County Down, in 1940. He was buried in the grounds of Stormont.

'...Hon. Member[s] must remember that in the South they boasted of a Catholic state. They still boast of Southern Ireland being a Catholic state.

All I boast of is that we are a Protestant Parliament and a Protestant state. It would be rather interesting for historians of the future to compare a Catholic state launched in the South with a Protestant state launched in the North and to see which gets on the better and prospers the more. It is most interesting for me at the moment to watch how they are progressing. I am doing my best always to top the bill and to be ahead of the South...

'We are a Protestant Parliament and a Protestant State.'

[Ulster people] shall not be impaired by people who come in here to help to break the last link between Great Britain and Ireland. They are attempting to do that in the South. That is an attempt to which we will be no party here. Therefore we are justified in taking all the steps we have taken in order to safeguard our position to the best of our ability. We have anticipated the British government because in our Civil Authorities Act we are able to deal with crime and outrage and threats just as strongly as the British government will be able to deal with the sowing of disaffection in His Majesty's forces.

'We shall not be impaired by people who come in here to help to break the last link between Great Britain and Ireland.'

I wish now to deal very shortly with the point that we can here quite readily and appropriately absorb our own natural increase in population from year to year. I think that industry, which is on the turn, will be able to pick up the unemployed of whom there are, I agree, far too many, some 63,000 in our midst. But I do not see why the loyal Ulster artisan should pay contributions in order to maintain people who come from the other side and who compete with them in the market here for labour, and until that 63,000 is fully absorbed it is only fair to place every obstacle we can in the way of people coming across the border from the Free State and after a certain time qualifying for taking the jobs of our people here.

'Employ only loyalists.'

I do claim that over and above law and order and the safety of the province there are strong arguments why we should protect our own loyal workingmen and if any preference is given they should be given that preference over anyone coming across the border. We have a long way to go yet. I think we should take every means as early as possible to urge the public to employ only loyalists. I say only loyalists. I do not care what their religion may be. I say as long as they are loyal people we will engage them and we will give them every chance and will help them, but we must be particular to see that none of these men can burrow underneath our constitution, working day and night to destroy Ulster, which took us so long to build up.

Before I close I would just like to say that fortunately for us there is no great hardship in the recommendation or advice which my right hon. friend gave.

I would ask the genial and kindly Member for South Fermanagh [Mr Healy] what hardship there will be if he uses his strong political influence to keep people in the

Free State and says to them, 'You who are not able to find work stay there. Do not come into Ulster. It is the most bigoted and horribly blackmouth place upon earth. Do not come in here. Stay in that glorious country, that part where it is overflowing with milk and honey, that new Jerusalem. Stay there and for God's sake do not put your noses across the border.'

'We will not hesitate for one moment to make safe and sure what we have.'

Surely an appeal of that sort would sink into the minds of the hon. Member's people. Let them all find their employment in their own area, and then we will have a better chance of picking up the unemployed upon the exchanges that already exist in the Ulster area. Let us be consistent in all these matters, and let us also never forget another matter, and this is of very great importance in the border counties. I do not suppose from the date that Mr Redmond on the one hand and Lord Carson and myself on the other hand attended the conference at Buckingham Palace, I do not suppose from that day to this that the counties of Tyrone and Fermanagh have ever been out of my mind. They must get all the support they ask for. They must get all the help they require, and so far as I am concerned and my colleagues in the government are concerned it will never be refused them. Never. I do not mind going a step further and saying that the government will be ready to pass even stronger legislation if it is found necessary to prevent anything I have hinted at today happening. We will not hesitate for one moment to make safe and sure what we have there and what we intend to hold (*hon. Members: 'Hear, hear'*).

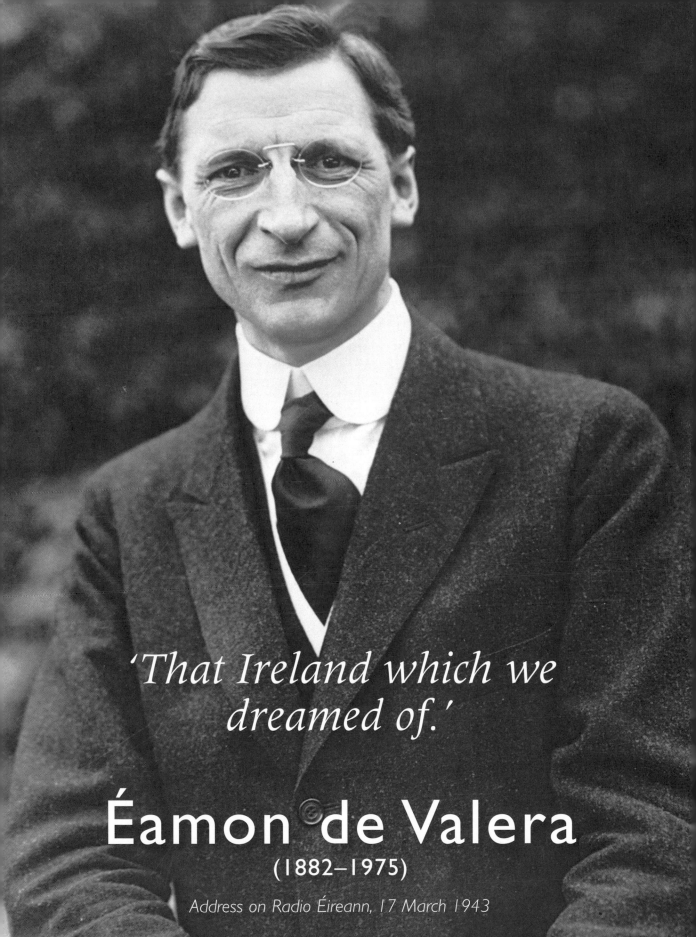

'*That Ireland which we dreamed of.*'

Éamon de Valera
(1882–1975)

Address on Radio Éireann, 17 March 1943

Though Éamon de Valera made many important speeches throughout a long career, he was often criticized as a poor orator. His slow delivery and clipped tone were far removed from the platform rabble-rousing and parliamentary grandstanding practised by so many of his generation. Yet as technology increasingly came to the fore in public life, so de Valera blossomed. The 'wireless' was an ideal match for his homely style of delivery, which seemed pitch perfect in the intimacy of 'front rooms' across Ireland.

In 1933, de Valera had officially opened a new high-powered radio station, capable of being heard throughout the country. He quickly recognized the significance of the medium not just in addressing the nation at home, but also in reaching out to the Irish abroad. His St Patrick's Day message of 1943 was one such event and proved to be among his most enduring statements.

This address coincided with the 50th anniversary of the Gaelic League, an organization that had been pivotal in shaping de Valera's own nationalist consciousness (as well as introducing him to his wife, Sineád Flanagan). It also commemorated the League's intellectual predecessors in Young Ireland. If it seems strange that de Valera chose to talk about such things in the middle of a world war, this was in keeping with the man. The revival of the Irish language and an end to partition remained his primary political objectives in all circumstances.

The cultural focus of this address, however, is less remembered than his portrayal of a rural idyll made up of 'cosy homesteads', 'sturdy children', 'athletic youths' and 'comely maidens'. (In recording the address, de Valera said 'happy maidens', but the phrase 'comely maidens' appeared in the official text.) Maybe there is something

BIOGRAPHY

Éamon de Valera was born in 1882 at Lexington Avenue, New York, the son of a Spanish artist father and an Irish mother. He moved in April 1885 to Ireland, where he was brought up on his uncle's farm in Bruree, County Limerick. Educated at Blackrock College, County Dublin, he took a BA degree from the Royal University in 1904. In 1913 de Valera enlisted in the Irish Volunteers and subsequently took part in the Easter Rising. He was the most senior figure not executed after the Rising. In 1917 he was elected MP for East Clare and, as leader of Sinn Féin, became president of Dáil Éireann until his resignation after the ratification of the Anglo-Irish Treaty in 1922. Interned during the civil war, he split with Sinn Féin over abstentionism in 1925 and founded Fianna Fáil the following year. De Valera was head of government in 1932–48, 1951–4 and 1957–9, and the president of Ireland in 1959–73. He died on 29 August 1975, just eight months after the death of his wife of 65 years, and was buried in Glasnevin Cemetery.

about conjuring such images – so clear and yet so sentimental – that makes them open to ridicule. (British prime minister John Major suffered a similar fate when he spoke affectionately of an England of warm beer, village greens and spinsters cycling to early morning communion).

Later the speech would become a byword for de Valera's supposed backwardness and patriarchal attitude towards women. Yet in the middle of the Emergency, with rationing in full sway, many responded positively to the call to forsake materialism in favour of loftier spiritual and cultural ideals.

Acutely conscious though we all are of the misery and desolation in which the greater part of the world is plunged, let us turn aside for a moment to that ideal Ireland that we would have.

'Fields and villages would be joyous with the sounds of industry.'

That Ireland which we dreamed of would be the home of a people who valued material wealth only as the basis of right living, of a people who were satisfied with frugal comfort and devoted their leisure to the things of the spirit – a land whose countryside would be bright with cosy homesteads – whose fields and villages would be joyous with the sounds of industry, with the romping of sturdy children, the contests of athletic youths and the laughter of comely maidens, whose firesides would be forums for the wisdom of serene old age. It would, in a word, be the home of a people living the life that God desires that man should live.

With the tidings that make such an Ireland possible, St Patrick came to our ancestors 1500 years ago, promising happiness here as well as happiness hereafter. It was the pursuit of such an Ireland that later made our country worthy to be called the Island of Saints and Scholars. It was the idea of such an Ireland, happy, vigorous, spiritual, that fired the imagination of our poets, that made successive generations of patriotic men give their lives to win religious and political liberty, and that will urge men in our own and future generations to die, if need be, so that these liberties may be preserved.

'It is to our nation as a whole that future must apply.'

One hundred years ago the Young Irelanders, by holding up the vision of such an Ireland before the people, inspired our nation and moved it spiritually as it had hardly been moved since the golden age of Irish civilization. Fifty years after the

Young Irelanders, the founders of the Gaelic League similarly inspired and moved the people of their day, as did later the leaders of the Volunteers. We of this time, if we have the will and the active enthusiasm, have the opportunity to inspire and move our generation in like manner. We can do so by keeping this thought of a noble future for our country constantly before our minds, ever seeking in action to bring that future into being, and ever remembering that it is to our nation as a whole that future must apply…

'The language is for us precious beyond measure.'

For many, the pursuit of the material is a necessity. Man, to express himself fully and to make the best use of the talents God has given him, needs a certain minimum of comfort and leisure. A section of our people have not yet this minimum. They rightly strive to secure it, and it must be our aim and the aim of all who are just and wise to assist in the effort. But many have got more than is required and are free, if they choose, to devote themselves more completely to cultivating the things of the mind, and in particular those which mark us out as a distinct nation.

The first of these latter is the national language. It is for us what no other language can be. It is our very own. It is more than a symbol; it is an essential part of our nationhood. It has been moulded by the thought of a hundred generations of our forebears. In it is stored the accumulated experience of a people, our people, who even before Christianity was brought to them were already cultured and living in a well-ordered society. The Irish language spoken in Ireland today is the direct descendant without break of the language our ancestors spoke in those far-off days.

'The task of restoring the language as the everyday speech of our people is a task as great as any nation ever undertook.'

As a vehicle of 3000 years of our history, the language is for us precious beyond measure. As the bearer to us of a philosophy, of an outlook on life deeply Christian and rich in practical wisdom, the language today is worth far too much to dream of letting it go. To part with it would be to abandon a great part of ourselves, to lose the key of our past, to cut away the roots from the tree. With the language gone we could never aspire again to being more than half a nation.

For my part, I believe that this outstanding mark of our nationhood can be preserved and made forever safe by this generation. I am indeed certain of it, but I know that it cannot be saved without understanding and co-operation and effort and sacrifice. It

'That Ireland which we dreamed of.'

would be wrong to minimize the difficulties. They are not slight. The task of restoring the language as the everyday speech of our people is a task as great as any nation ever undertook. But it is a noble task. Other nations have succeeded in it, though in their case, when the effort was begun, their national language was probably more widely spoken among their people than is ours with us. As long as the language lives, however, on the lips of the people as their natural speech in any substantial part of this land we are assured of success if – *if* we are in earnest …

Bail ó Dhia oraibh agus bail go gcuire Sé ar an obair atá romhainn. Go gcumhdaí Dia sinn agus gur fiú sinn choíche, mar náisiún, na tiolacaí a thug Pádraig chugainn. Go dtuga an tUilechumhachtach, A thug slán sinn go dtí seo ón anachain is ón mi-ádh atá ar oiread sin náisiún eile de bharr an chogaidh seo, scáth agus didean dúinn go dtí an deireadh, agus go ndeonaí Sé gur fiú sinn cion uasal a dhéanamh sa saol nua atá romhainn. ['God bless you and bless the work that lies before us. May God protect us, and may we always, as a nation, be worthy of the gifts that St Patrick brought us. May the Almighty, Who has brought us safe until now from the calamity and misfortune that have befallen so many other nations in consequence of this war, grant us shelter and protection to the end and make us worthy to play a noble part in the new world of the future.']

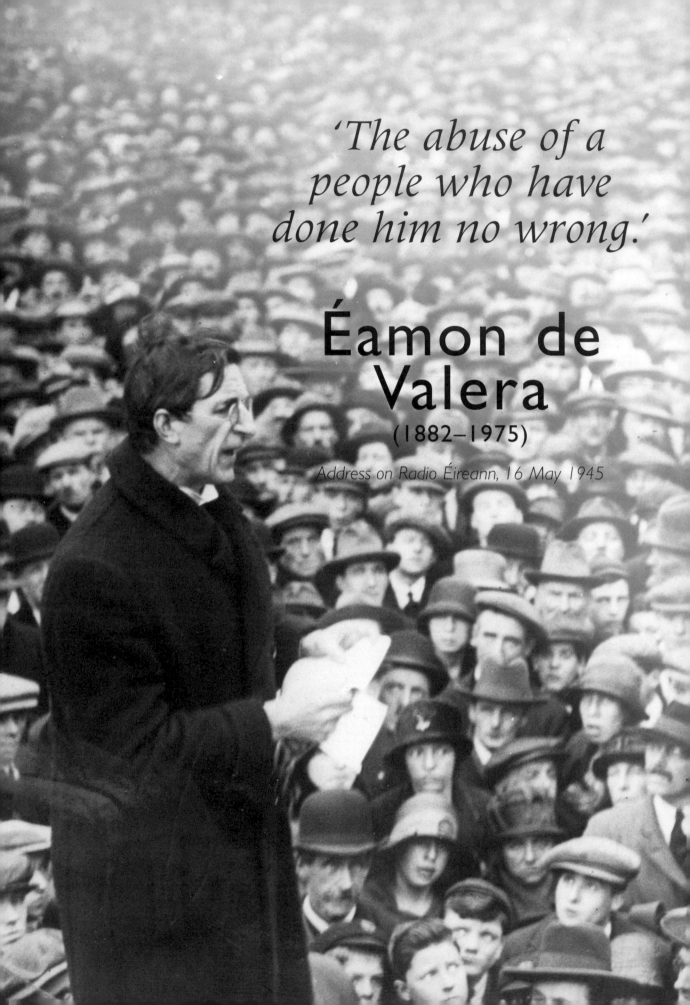

'The abuse of a people who have done him no wrong.'

Éamon de Valera
(1882–1975)

Address on Radio Éireann, 16 May 1945

'The abuse of a people who have done him no wrong.'

When war broke out in Europe in 1939, the taoiseach Éamon de Valera declared that Ireland would remain neutral. There was unanimity among politicians of all hues (with the notable exception of deputy James Dillon) and most of the public at large that neutrality was in the national interest. Still, while the government outwardly observed neutrality to the point of absurdity (a photograph of a government minister ice skating on a frozen lake was banned in case it revealed climatic conditions to any of the belligerents) and even to offence (de Valera's notorious courtesy visit to the German legation in Dublin on the death of Hitler), the truth remained that Ireland was neutral in name only. Ireland provided behind-the-scenes support for the Allies in a variety of ways, particularly through intelligence, which included the crucial weather report that allowed D-Day to proceed.

In May 1945 Winston Churchill spoke on the BBC to mark his fifth anniversary as prime minister. He outlined the tasks ahead in defeating Japan and reflected on the circumstances that had led to victory that month in Europe. In the midst of this, he made a trenchant personal attack on de Valera for his determination to keep Ireland out of the war.

'Owing to the action of Mr de Valera,' Churchill asserted, 'so much at variance with the temper and instinct of thousands of southern Irishmen, who hastened to the battle-front to prove their ancient valour, the approaches which the southern Irish ports and airfields could so easily have guarded were closed by hostile aircrafts and U-boats.' Under the circumstances, said the prime minister, Ireland was lucky to avoid military conflict with Britain. 'With a restraint and poise to which, I say, history will find few parallels,' maintained Churchill, 'we never laid a violent hand upon them, which at times would have been quite easy and quite natural, and left the de Valera government to frolic with the German and later with the Japanese representatives to their heart's content.'

The speech enjoyed favourable publicity around the world, not least in the United States, where it was broadcast in full and reported on at length. The *New York Herald Tribune*, for example, praised Churchill for clarifying 'the real extent of Mr de Valera's peculiar contribution to history and the narrow margin by which German secret weapons failed to inflict disaster.'

De Valera's reply on 16 May was the finest speech he ever made. A measured but forceful argument adroitly matched Churchill's righteous indignation. A man who so often divided opinion on this occasion spoke for the nation. Less obvious at the time was de Valera's acknowledgment that in earlier days he would have added 'fuel to the flames of hatred and passion'. It was a moment of self-awareness that perhaps hinted at de Valera's recognition of his own role in Ireland's traumatic past.

Certain newspapers have been very persistent in looking for my answer to Mr Churchill's recent broadcast. I know the kind of answer I am expected to make. I know the answer that first springs to the lips of every man of Irish blood who heard or read that speech, no matter in what circumstances or in what part of the world he found himself.

I know the reply I would have given a quarter of a century ago. But I have deliberately decided that that is not the reply I shall make tonight. I shall strive not to be guilty of adding any fuel to the flames of hatred and passion which, if continued to be fed, promise to burn up whatever is left by the war of decent human feeling in Europe.

'There are some things which it is my duty to say.'

Allowances can be made for Mr Churchill's statement, however unworthy, in the first flush of his victory. No such excuse could be found for me in this quieter atmosphere. There are, however, some things which it is my duty to say, some things which it is essential to say. I shall try to say them as dispassionately as I can.

Mr Churchill makes it clear that, in certain circumstances, he would have violated our neutrality and that he would justify his action by Britain's necessity. It seems strange to me that Mr Churchill does not see that this, if accepted, would mean that Britain's necessity would become a moral code and that when this necessity became sufficiently great, other people's rights were not to count.

It is quite true that other great powers believe in this same code – in their own regard – and have behaved in accordance with it. That is precisely why we have the disastrous succession of wars – World War no. 1 and World War no. 2 – and shall it be World War no. 3?

Surely Mr Churchill must see that, if his contention be admitted in our regard, a like justification can be framed for similar acts of aggression elsewhere and no small nation adjoining a great power could ever hope to be permitted to go its own way in peace.

'It is, indeed, hard for the strong to be just to the weak.'

It is, indeed, fortunate that Britain's necessity did not reach the point when Mr Churchill would have acted. All credit to him that he successfully resisted the temptation which, I have no doubt, many times assailed him in his difficulties and to which I freely admit many leaders might have easily succumbed. It is, indeed, hard for the strong to be just to the weak, but acting justly always has its rewards.

By resisting his temptation in this instance, Mr Churchill, instead of adding another horrid chapter to the already bloodstained record of the relations between England and this country, has advanced the cause of international morality an important step – one of the most important, indeed, that can be taken on the road to the establishment of any sure basis for peace.

As far as the peoples of these two islands are concerned, it may, perhaps, mark a fresh beginning towards the realization of that mutual comprehension to which Mr Churchill has referred and for which he has prayed and for which, I hope, he will not merely pray but work, also, as did his predecessor [Neville Chamberlain] who will yet, I believe, find the honoured place in British history which is due to him, as certainly he will find it in any fair record of the relations between Britain and ourselves.

That Mr Churchill should be irritated when our neutrality stood in the way of what he thought he vitally needed, I understand, but that he or any thinking person in Britain or elsewhere should fail to see the reason for our neutrality, I find it hard to conceive.

'Suppose Germany had won the war.'

I would like to put a hypothetical question – it is a question I have put to many Englishmen since the last war. Suppose Germany had won the war, had invaded and occupied England, and that after a long lapse of time and many bitter struggles she was finally brought to acquiesce in admitting England's right to freedom, and let England go, but not the whole of England, all but, let us say, the six southern counties.

These six southern counties, those, let us suppose, commanding the entrance to the narrow seas, Germany had singled out and insisted on holding herself with a view to weakening England as a whole and maintaining the security of her own communications through the Straits of Dover.

Let us suppose, further, that after all this had happened Germany was engaged in a great war in which she could show that she was on the side of the freedom of a number of small nations. Would Mr Churchill as an Englishman who believed that his own nation had as good a right to freedom as any other – not freedom for a part merely, but freedom for the whole – would he, whilst Germany still maintained the partition of his country and occupied six counties of it, would he lead this partitioned England to join with Germany in a crusade? I do not think Mr Churchill would.

Would he think the people of partitioned England an object of shame if they stood neutral in such circumstances? I do not think Mr Churchill would.

Mr Churchill is proud of Britain's stand alone, after France had fallen and before America entered the war.

Could he not find in his heart the generosity to acknowledge that there is a small nation that stood alone, not for one year or two, but for several hundred years against aggression; that endured spoliations, famines, massacres in endless succession; that was clubbed many times into insensibility, but that each time, on returning consciousness, took up the fight anew; a small nation that could never be got to accept defeat and has never surrendered her soul?

'We too will strive to be faithful to the end.'

Mr Churchill is justly proud of his nation's perseverance against heavy odds. But we in this island are still prouder of our people's perseverance for freedom through all the centuries. We of our time have played our part in that perseverance, and we have pledged ourselves to the dead generations who have preserved intact for us this glorious heritage, that we too will strive to be faithful to the end, and pass on this tradition unblemished.

Many a time in the past there appeared little hope except that hope to which Mr Churchill referred, that by standing fast a time would come when, to quote his own words, 'the tyrant would make some ghastly mistake which would alter the whole balance of the struggle.'

I sincerely trust, however, that it is not thus our ultimate unity and freedom will be achieved, though as a younger man I confess I prayed even for that, and indeed at times saw no other.

'The present excuse for continuing the injustice of the mutilation of our country.'

In latter years I have had a vision of a nobler and better ending, better for both our peoples and for the future of mankind. For that I have now been long working. I regret that it is not to this nobler purpose that Mr Churchill is lending his hand rather than by the abuse of a people who have done him no wrong, trying to find in a crisis like the present excuse for continuing the injustice of the mutilation of our country.

I sincerely hope that Mr Churchill has not deliberately chosen the latter course but, if he has, however regretfully we may say it, we can only say, be it so …

'The honesty of my motives
will be attacked by able men.'

Noël Browne
(1915–97)

Statement to Dáil Éireann, 12 April 1951

The crisis surrounding the 'Mother and Child' scheme was one of the most notorious episodes in the politics of independent Ireland. In 1947, the Fianna Fáil government had passed a far-reaching Health Act that included provision for free ante- and post-natal health care for mothers, and free health care for children under 16. This 'Mother and Child' scheme was opposed by two powerful vested interests: doctors and the Catholic church. Medics feared it was the first step towards a centralized National Health Service. The church argued that state intervention was contrary to Catholic social teaching and would encourage indolence. Legal delays meant the scheme was never implemented in the government's lifetime.

In March 1948 the first inter-party government came to power. It was a coalition made up of seven different political groups spanning the ideological spectrum. The new minister for health, Noël Browne, was appointed on his first day in the Dáil, aged just 32. He was an enthusiastic minister, who earned plaudits for his success in tackling the problem of tuberculosis. Yet his inexperience as a politician showed in the attempts to implement a modified version of the 'Mother and Child' welfare scheme. The same powerful interest groups were again to the fore. Doctors combined with the Catholic hierarchy to mount a campaign of opposition.

The minister was a devout Catholic who 'unequivocally and unreservedly' accepted the views of the church. He asked the Catholic hierarchy for a specific ruling on whether the 'Mother and Child' scheme contradicted Catholic moral teaching. A reply came back that it was contrary to Catholic *social* teaching. Believing this to be a vital distinction, he pushed ahead with the scheme only to find that the Cabinet would not back him. On 11 April 1951 Browne reluctantly resigned.

Browne handed correspondence relating to the controversy to the *Irish Times*. This lifted the lid on behind-the-scenes campaigning by the hierarchy to influence the government. The members of the Cabinet other than Browne, writes J.H. Whyte, 'looked like men who did not have the courage of their convictions'. Seen by many as proof of the malign influence of the church, the correspondence caused uproar on both sides of the border. Browne and several other deputies withdrew

BIOGRAPHY

Noël Browne was born in 1915 and educated by the Jesuits at Beaumont College, London, and at Trinity College, Dublin. After his family was ravaged by tuberculosis, he was taken in by the wealthy family of a schoolfriend, who paid for his medical studies at university. After qualifying as a doctor in 1940, he specialized in TB. Asked by Clann na Poblachta to stand in the 1948 general election, Browne became a minister on his first day in Dáil Éireann. Over the course of a quixotic career he was a member of five political parties. His 1986 memoir, *Against the Tide*, became Ireland's bestselling autobiography. Browne died at Baile na hAbhann, County Galway, in 1997.

'The honesty of my motives will be attacked by able men.'

their support for the coalition, which fell a month later on the notional issue of the price of milk.

In this resignation statement to the Dáil on 12 April 1951, Browne fearlessly set out the circumstances surrounding the 'Mother and Child' crisis. In doing so, he won a place in the liberal pantheon.

I have pledged myself to the public and to the Clann na Poblachta Party to introduce a mother and child health scheme which would not embody a means test. Since I could not succeed in fulfilling my promise in this regard I consider it my duty to vacate my office.

'I have not been able to accept the manner in which this matter has been dealt with.'

While, as I have said, I as a Catholic accept unequivocally and unreservedly the views of the hierarchy on this matter, I have not been able to accept the manner in which this matter has been dealt with by my former colleagues in the government.

In June 1948, the government, in Cabinet, authorized me to introduce a mother and child health scheme to provide free maternity treatment for mothers and free treatment for their children up to the age of 16 years … On 10 October 1950, I was informed that His Grace the Archbishop of Dublin, wished to see me in connection with the proposed scheme. I attended at the Archbishop's House on the following day where I met His Grace and Their Lordships, the Bishops of Ferns and Galway. I was informed that at a meeting of the hierarchy on the previous day at Maynooth, His Grace and Their Lordships had been appointed to put before the government certain objections which the hierarchy saw in the scheme; that I was being informed of these objections as a matter of courtesy before transmission to the taoiseach as head of the government …

About the 9th or 10th of November I learned that the taoiseach had received a letter, dated 10 October 1950, from the Bishop of Ferns, as secretary to the hierarchy. The taoiseach gave me this letter for my observations with a view to a reply. The objections in the letter appeared to be those read to me by His Grace the Archbishop of Dublin, during my interview on 11 October, and, in the light of the later events, I concluded that it had been transmitted solely for the purpose of record and formal reply. I, therefore, acting on this assumption, prepared a draft letter for transmission by the taoiseach to His Lordship of Ferns, as secretary to the hierarchy, in reply to the various points raised in their letter. In this answer I substantially recapitulated the case I had made when I met His Grace and Their Lordships at Drumcondra on

11 October. I would like to emphasize that, as I still believed that His Grace and Their Lordships had been reassured by the case made by me on 11 October, I merely regarded this reply also as being for purposes of record by the hierarchy. I sent this draft to the taoiseach shortly after mid-November to be forwarded by him to the hierarchy. As I heard nothing further about the matter from either the hierarchy or the taoiseach until a couple of weeks ago I had no reason to believe that the hierarchy were not fully satisfied, and the work of preparing for the introduction of the mother and child scheme continued ... and on 6 March its early implementation was widely publicized by me ...

On 9 March I received a letter from His Grace the Archbishop of Dublin. From this letter I was surprised to learn that His Grace might not approve of the scheme, and declared that the objections which had been raised by him in October had not been resolved. I was surprised for the simple reason that I had heard nothing further, either from His Grace the Archbishop of Dublin, acting on behalf of the hierarchy, or from the taoiseach, acting for the government, in the four months that had intervened since I had handed to the taoiseach in November my reply to Their Lordships' letter. Following receipt of His Grace's letter, a copy of which was sent by His Grace to the taoiseach, the latter suggested to me on 15 March that I should take steps at once to consult the hierarchy regarding their objections to the scheme. I then learned to my distress and amazement that the reply to Their Lordships' letter which I had prepared and sent to the taoiseach in the previous November had, in fact, never been sent by him ...

'Their Lordships' objections were still unresolved.'

I told the taoiseach orally that his failure to forward this reply had placed me in a very embarrassing position and might easily give Their Lordships the impression that I had omitted to give any consideration to their objections and that further I had been guilty of extreme discourtesy in failing to ensure that a reply had been sent to them. I also pointed out that his failure to send this letter had the effect that I remained under the erroneous impression that the objections of the hierarchy had been fully resolved and that I could proceed with the scheme. I was surprised also to learn from the taoiseach that he had been in constant communication with His Grace the Archbishop of Dublin on this matter since the receipt of the letter of 10 October from the hierarchy, so presumably he was fully aware that Their Lordships' objections were still unresolved. He offered no explanation as to why, in the light of this knowledge, he had failed to keep me informed of the position; had allowed me continuously to refer in public speeches to the scheme as decided and unchanged government policy, and finally had allowed the scheme to go ahead to the point where it had been advertised at considerable public expense and had been announced to the public, both in these advertisements and by my radio talk ...

'The honesty of my motives will be attacked by able men.'

The letter sent by the taoiseach on 27 March 1951, to the Bishop of Ferns, in his capacity as secretary to the hierarchy, enclosing my observations, refers to the scheme 'advocated by the minister for health', thereby implying that the scheme was not advocated or supported by himself or other members of the government. In a letter of 5 April from His Grace the Archbishop of Dublin, written on behalf of the hierarchy, it is stated that they were pleased to note that no evidence had been supplied in the taoiseach's letter of 27 March that the proposed mother and child scheme advocated by the minister for health enjoys the support of the government. I have, accordingly, regretfully come to the conclusion that, notwithstanding the government decision of June 1948 against the inclusion of a means test, the taoiseach and the other members of the government had, in fact, changed their minds about the scheme.

It is a fact noted by many people that in no public speeches did ministers of the government other than myself speak in favour of this measure. I regret that for the want of courage on their part they should have allowed the scheme to progress so very far – that they should have failed to keep me informed of the true position in regard to their own attitude and the attitude of others. I have, consequently, been allowed by their silence to commit myself to the country to implement a scheme which certain members of the government at least did not want, on their own admission, to see implemented and which they were in fact aware could not be implemented.

I trust that the standards manifested in these dealings are not customary in the public life of this or any other democratic nation and I hope that my experience has been exceptional.

'My aims will be called in question.'

I have not lightly decided to take the course I have taken. I know the consequences which may follow my action. The honesty of my motives will be attacked by able men; my aims will be called in question; ridicule and doubt will be cast upon the wisdom of my insistence in striving to realize the declared objectives of the party to which I belonged.

As minister for health I was enabled to make some progress in improving the health services of the nation only because I received the generous co-operation of members of all political parties and of all sections of the community. I lay down my seal of office content that you – Members of this House – and the people who are our masters here, shall judge whether I have striven to honour the trust placed on me.

'100,000 jobs.'

Seán Lemass

(1899–1971)

Speech at Clery's ballroom, Dublin, 11 October 1955

'100,000 jobs.'

The 1950s was a bleak decade for Ireland. Most of western Europe had seen postwar austerity give way to an age of affluence. Not so Ireland. The cost of living, unemployment and emigration figures were all sky-high. Some 40,000 people a year were leaving the country. The 1955 census showed the population of the Republic at its lowest-ever level. This was not merely an economic crisis, but one of national confidence. Protesters were marching through the streets of Dublin. The country's leaders showed little sense of knowing how to stop the downward spiral. Three different governments had been elected between 1948 and 1954. Each one seemed worse than the last.

In 1955, with Fianna Fáil out of office, Seán Lemass began searching for a big idea to shake up the economy. Lemass was a pragmatic nationalist. As minister for industry and commerce in the 1930s, he had shielded the Irish economy behind a raft of tariff barriers. Now he concluded this policy, which had become economic orthodoxy, was failing Ireland. To find a way forward, he studied European examples of economic planning, particularly Italy's ten-year employment and income scheme (the Vanoni Plan), and consulted progressive public servants such as 'Todd' Andrews and Ken Whitaker.

When Lemass presented his own plan to Fianna Fáil it led to dramatic clashes with colleagues, notably Seán MacEntee. On 11 October 1955 he gambled by making his ideas public at a party meeting at Clery's ballroom in Dublin. The speech was published afterwards as a four-page supplement in the *Irish Press*. Lemass's promise to create 100,000 jobs in five years attracted huge attention. By the time the Costello government collapsed in early 1957, Fianna Fáil, despite its initial caution, had adopted the Clery's agenda. The party swept home at a general election fought on economic issues. In 1958 Lemass launched the first programme for economic development. The following year he succeeded de Valera as taoiseach.

> **BIOGRAPHY**
>
> **Seán Lemass** was born John Francis Lemass in Ballybrack, County Dublin, in 1899 to a Catholic family of Huguenot origins. He abandoned his education to join the Irish Volunteers, becoming one of the youngest participants in the Easter Rising. He was active in the war of independence and took the anti-Treaty side in the civil war, during which his brother Noel was tortured and killed by Free State soldiers. Lemass sided with de Valera over the split with Sinn Féin in 1925 and became a founder of Fianna Fáil. Elected to Dáil Éireann in 1927, he served in all de Valera's governments and succeeded him as taoiseach in 1959. His resignation due to ill health in 1966 caused widespread shock. Lemass died in Dublin in 1971 and was buried at Dean's Grange Cemetery.

Lemass's Clery's address signalled one of the most important policy U-turns in the history of the state. It also offered an example of a speech that was seminal without even reaching the foothills let alone the heights of oratorical eloquence.

The FF party has accepted the conclusion that the economic development programme which it initiated 25 years ago, notwithstanding its many and very substantial achievements and its subsequent acceptance by all political parties, has not proved to be sufficient to bring about all the economic and social progress which we desired and which we believe can be accomplished.

We have used this present period of release from immediate responsibility for government in reviewing our programme and preparing new plans so that under FF leadership, the nation can experience another era of advancement. The proposals which I am about to outline when completed will form an integral part of these plans.

Briefly, these proposals are based on the view that the successful application of a sound development policy requires an adequate and carefully prepared investment programme and will depend on the country's capacity to execute such a programme and that this investment programme must in its earlier stages be undertaken mainly by the government.

We do not believe, however, that Irish progress and prosperity can be secured by government action alone, and an essential part of the proposals are therefore concerned with the promotion of a sufficient and expanding volume of investment on private account …

'The effort needed is not beyond the country's possibilities.'

The aims of the proposals are, firstly, to give the national economy the necessary initial boost; secondly, to bring about an increase in private investment activity to the extent required to secure an adequate and continuing expansion of the scope and efficiency of private productive enterprise; and thirdly, to show that the effort needed is not beyond the country's possibilities.

The main proposal is that as a first step to the attainment of full employment, the government should undertake a positive spending programme spread over a five-year period. This should be financed otherwise than by taxation or by borrowing from current savings and planned on a scale estimated to be sufficient, taking into account the volume of private activity, to raise total national outlay – private consumption spending, plus private business investment, plus public authority expenditure – to a level calculated to be adequate to set up a demand for the whole of the labour available for employment.

In conjunction with that programme of investment expenditure, other measures must also be adopted to increase the volume of savings and to direct these savings to investment in Ireland to an extent that will ensure, in subsequent years, a satisfactory economic and social position without abnormal government support.

In other words, our view is that the government must carry the main burden in the first instance, but must so arrange its programme that it can gradually fade out of the picture, leaving private economic activity the main basis of national prosperity.

It is clear that the scale of the public expenditure which will be required to bring national outlay to full employment level within five years will be very considerable. FF rejects the view which is sometimes propagated in a section of the press and elsewhere, that the sole object of government policy should be to keep public expenditure at the lowest possible level. The primary aims of FF's policy have been in the past, and will always be, to increase the nation's wealth and to improve the living conditions of the people. These aims over-ride other considerations ...

On the average during the year, 8.1 per cent of ... workers were unemployed. Since 1946, the total labour force has declined by 61,000, that is at an annual rate of over 7500 persons or 0.6 per cent per annum. Net emigration averages about 25,000 per year of which from one half to two thirds may be assumed to be preventable in the sense that a fair prospect of security of employment in Ireland would keep that number from emigrating.

'An increase over five years in the number of jobs by 100,000.'

It is safe to assume, however, that an increase over five years in the number of jobs by 100,000 or an average rate of increase of 20,000 per year would result in full employment as ordinarily understood and the end of abnormal emigration. Indeed, this calculation may exaggerate the position, but it is wiser to plan on an adequate rather than an inadequate scale. At the end of the five years, 15,000 new jobs per annum should enable full employment to be maintained ...

The proposals which I have outlined can do no more than ensure that the efforts of the Irish people to improve their living conditions, to end unemployment and to reduce emigration will be facilitated by a proper disposal of national resources and not impeded by their partial immobilization as at present.

They are put forward in the belief that this country's inability to achieve the same employment conditions and living standards as other small west European countries is due solely to the circumstances which have prevented the full utilization of available resources and not to any incapacity of the Irish people to accomplish the same productive effort as these other countries have achieved.

It is along these lines that FF is planning the nation's future progress. In the present task of completing these plans and the ultimate task of fulfilling them, FF asks the co-operation and support of all sections of the Irish people.

'No one is likely to dispute the existence or the gravity of these dangers.'

Frank Aiken

(1898–1983)

Speech to the United Nations General Assembly, 17 October 1958

*'No one is likely to dispute the existence or
the gravity of these dangers.'*

Ireland joined the United Nations in 1956. Liam Cosgrave, minister for external affairs in the second inter-party government, promised to 'do whatever we can as a member ... to preserve the Christian civilization of which we are a part, and to support whenever possible those powers principally responsible for the defences of the free world in their resistance to the spread of Communist power.' This led to some awkward moments. In his first address to the assembly, Cosgrave called upon Jews and Arabs to settle their differences on Christian principles. 'It may not be all that appropriate for the Middle East,' wryly observed the civil servant Freddie Boland, 'but the minister feels it will go down well in Dun Laoghaire/Rathdown [his constituency].'

This initial stance inevitably meant following America's lead. An election the following year brought a fundamental shift in position. Frank Aiken, minister for external affairs in the new Fianna Fáil government, was deeply suspicious of the United States. As the minister responsible for national defence during the Second World War, he had borne the brunt of US hostility over neutrality. His republicanism, moreover, meant that his natural sympathies lay with the post-colonial societies that had emerged after the war. Ireland had been too subservient to the United States, he believed, and should follow a more independent line. It was an attitude that 'often irritated the United States,' says Eunan O'Halpin, 'but undoubtedly enhanced the country's standing in the international community.'

Aiken's most enduring contribution to international affairs was the Irish non-proliferation treaty. He first put this before the assembly on 17 October 1958. An amended version was agreed in 1961 and became UN resolution 1665 – the so-called 'Irish resolution'.

BIOGRAPHY

Frank Aiken was born in Camlough, County Armagh, in 1898 to a prosperous farming family. Educated in Newry by the Christian Brothers, he joined the Irish Volunteers at 16 and commanded a division of the Irish Republican Army (IRA) during the war of independence. Although an anti-Treaty supporter in 1922, he made strenuous efforts to prevent division and civil war. Aiken succeeded Liam Lynch as chief of staff of the IRA in March 1923; two months later he issued the ceasefire and dump arms orders that effectively ended the civil war. He served in the first Fianna Fáil government as minister for defence (1932–9), later becoming minister for the co-ordination of defensive measures (1939–45), minister for finance (1945–8) and minister for external affairs (1951–4, 1957–69). Aiken died in Dublin in 1983 and was buried in Camlough, County Armagh.

An important factor in this changing world situation today – a factor to which I referred in my speech in the general debate in the Assembly and to which several speakers, including the distinguished representative of India, have also referred – is the imminent danger that more and more states will come to possess nuclear weapons. My delegation considers it necessary to focus attention on this problem.

With this in mind we have submitted certain amendments to the draft resolution of the 17 powers. We have also tabled a draft resolution.

'It should remain in being until the total abolition of nuclear weapons renders it superfluous.'

The amendments and the resolution are in the hands of the committee. The amendments, if accepted, would urge the non-nuclear powers, during a specified period, to refrain from manufacturing or acquiring nuclear weapons and would urge the nuclear powers to refrain from supplying such weapons to states which do not now possess them. We have specified a period of time in order to co-ordinate our proposals with those in the 17-power resolution, and in the hope of attracting the widest possible measure of acceptance. But we have no wish to conceal the fact that we regard the proposed temporary measure of nuclear restriction as only a step towards a permanent ban on the further dissemination of nuclear weapons – permanent in the sense that it should remain in being until the total abolition of nuclear weapons renders it superfluous. Similarly in the case of our draft resolution, which proposes an *ad hoc* commission to study the problem of the dissemination of nuclear weapons, it is our hope and belief that this study would lead to a permanent ban on such dissemination. Both our amendments and our draft resolution, therefore, are conceived as steps towards the restriction of nuclear weapons – a restriction which in its turn would be a step towards their abolition.

The first point I wish to stress, Mr Chairman, is that as this committee, and the great powers represented in it, are unable speedily to abolish nuclear weapons completely, they ought at least, in our opinion, to take steps aimed at preventing the threat from becoming even greater. It is, in our opinion, a great tragedy that the Baruch proposals for the international control of nuclear weapons and nuclear development were not accepted and implemented 12 years ago. If we do not soon succeed in limiting the number of states making or possessing nuclear weapons, the problem of saving the world from nuclear destruction may well have passed beyond the power of man to solve long before another 12 years have passed.

'This weapon will pass into the hands of states with much less to lose.'

'No one is likely to dispute the existence or
the gravity of these dangers.'

The danger of nuclear weapons to humanity, it seems to us, does not merely increase in direct ratio to the number of those possessing them. It seems likely to increase in geometric progression. Those who now possess nuclear weapons are a few great and highly developed states, with great urban populations, with much to lose and little to gain in a nuclear war. Their potential adversaries are in the same case and have the power to retaliate. As in the case of every other military invention, however, the harnessing of nuclear energy for military purposes is bound to become simpler and cheaper with the passing of time. Sooner or later, therefore, unless this organization takes urgent preventive steps, this weapon will pass into the hands of states with much less to lose. Furthermore, as it comes into their hands, it may give them a temporary but enormous advantage over their adversaries – an advantage which they will be sorely tempted to exploit.

'One obsolete, Hiroshima-type bomb … could be the detonator for worldwide thermonuclear war.'

We can all think, Mr Chairman, of several regions of the world where fierce antagonisms exist, held in suspense only by a kind of truce or deadlock. That truce, that deadlock, could be broken all too easily if one side or the other possessed nuclear weapons. In short, the nuclear stalemate ceases to apply once nuclear weapons begin to come into the hands of the smaller countries. Furthermore, nothing except international measures to prevent the dissemination of such weapons can prevent them from coming, ultimately, not merely to small and poor states but also to revolutionary organizations. All through history portable weapons which are the monopoly of the great powers today become the weapons of smaller powers and revolutionary groups tomorrow. And since local wars and revolutions almost always involve some degree of great power patronage and rivalry, the use of nuclear weapons by a small state or revolutionary group could lead, only too easily, to the outbreak of general war. One obsolete, Hiroshima-type bomb, used by a small and desperate country to settle a local quarrel, could be the detonator for worldwide thermonuclear war, involving the destruction of our whole civilization.

I do not think it necessary to emphasize further the dangers which will arise if nuclear weapons become more widespread. No one is likely to dispute the existence or the gravity of these dangers …

Kennedy stands with relatives on a visit to Dunganstown

'*Ireland's hour has come.*'

John F. Kennedy
(1917–63)

Speech to the Joint Houses of the Oireachtas, 28 June 1963

'Ireland's hour has come.'

John F. Kennedy was the personification of American glamour and power. For the people of Ireland, he was much more. This second-generation Irish-American – the first Catholic to be elected president of the United States – represented a triumph of the Irish abroad. The boy was 'one of ours'. And he'd 'done good'.

In the 1960 US election, Kennedy had played down his Irish-American background lest it draw attention to his Catholicism. By 1963, this looked unlikely to feature in the following year's re-election campaign, so Kennedy added Ireland to his itinerary for a visit to Europe.

The first serving president of the United States to visit independent Ireland, his trip in June 1963 was an event of huge symbolic importance. Kennedy arrived in a country that was more confident and prosperous than at any time since 1921. The depression that had characterized the 1950s, when Irish society had been ravaged by unemployment and mass emigration, had passed. The Fianna Fáil government of Seán Lemass had liberalized the Irish economy by lifting import barriers and encouraging foreign direct investment. Ireland seemed to have turned a corner.

Lemass saw in the presidential visit an opportunity to divest Ireland of its shamrocks and shillelaghs image. Instead, the taoiseach wanted to present the country to the world as dynamic, modern and industrialized.

He did not stand a chance. The American media, led by Walter Cronkite on CBS, was firmly wedded to the 'fighting Irish', turf-sods on a donkey, John Hinde picture-postcard view of Ireland. The Lemass economic 'miracle' barely got a mention. Even Kennedy referred to it only in passing. His visit had been organized to bolster support at home, so he delivered a speech on 28 June that extolled traditional Irish-American values. Perhaps it was for this reason that Lemass disliked Kennedy, whom he found cold and calculating.

For everyone else, Kennedy's was a bravura performance. His meticulously researched and beautifully written speech delivered to the Oireachtas proved a hit both with the Irish at home and Irish-Americans. As one of those present that day later recalled, 'Kennedy gave a consummate performance, and his

BIOGRAPHY

John F. Kennedy was born in 1917 in Brookline, Massachusetts, into an Irish-American family. His millionaire father, Joseph P. Kennedy, served as US ambassador to London in 1938–40. Educated at Harvard, JFK joined the navy in 1940 and became a war hero following the PT109 incident. Elected to the House of Representatives after the war and subsequently to the Senate, he won the Pulitzer Prize in 1957 for *Profiles in Courage*. In 1960 he won a closely contested election, becoming the first Catholic US president and commander-in-chief. Kennedy was killed by a sniper's bullet in Dallas on 22 November 1963 and was buried in Arlington National Cemetery. His funeral, the focus of worldwide attention, was presided over by Cardinal Cushing of Boston, a first-generation Irish-American.

audience lay spellbound and mesmerized by his professionalism ... The overwhelming majority of the people in Ireland enjoyed what he said and admired him for saying it.' It was the moment the Irish diaspora came home.

Mr Speaker, Prime Minister, Members of the Parliament: I am grateful for your welcome and for that of your countrymen.

The 13th day of December, 1862, will be a day long remembered in American history. At Fredericksburg, Virginia, thousands of men fought and died on one of the bloodiest battlefields of the American Civil War. One of the most brilliant stories of that day was written by a band of 1200 men who went into battle wearing a green sprig in their hats. They bore a proud heritage and a special courage, given to those who had long fought for the cause of freedom. I am referring, of course, to the Irish Brigade. As General Robert E. Lee, the great military leader of the Southern Confederate forces, was reported to have said of this group of men after the battle, 'The gallant stand which this bold brigade made on the heights of Fredericksburg is well known. Never were men so brave. They ennobled their race by their splendid gallantry on that desperate occasion. Their brilliant, though hopeless, assaults on our lines excited the hearty applause of our officers and soldiers.'

'Never were men so brave.'

Of the 1200 men who took part in that assault, 280 survived the battle. The Irish Brigade was led into battle on that occasion by Brigadier-General Thomas F. Meagher, who had participated in the unsuccessful Irish uprising of 1848, was captured by the British and sent in a prison ship to Australia, from whence he finally came to America. In the fall of 1862, after serving with distinction and gallantry in some of the toughest fighting of this most bloody struggle, the Irish Brigade was presented with a new set of flags. In the city ceremony, the city chamberlain gave them the motto 'The Union, our Country, and Ireland Forever'. Their old ones having been torn to shreds by bullets in previous battles, Captain Richard McGee took possession of these flags on September 2nd in New York City and arrived with them at the Battle of Fredericksburg and carried them in the battle. Today, in recognition of what these gallant Irishmen and what millions of other Irish have done for my country, and through the generosity of the Fighting 69th, I would like to present one of these flags to the people of Ireland.

As you can see, gentlemen [sic], the battle honours of the brigade include Fredericksburg, Chancellorsville, Yorktown, Fair Oaks, Gaines Mill, Allen's Farm, Savage's Station, White Oak Bridge, Glendale, Malvern Hill, Antietam, Gettysburg, and Bristow Station.

'I am proud to be the first American president to visit Ireland during his term of office.'

I am deeply honoured to be your guest in the free Parliament of a free Ireland. If this nation had achieved its present political and economic stature a century or so ago, my great-grandfather might never have left New Ross, and I might, if fortunate, be sitting down there with you. Of course, if your own President [de Valera] had never left Brooklyn, he might be standing up here instead of me ...

I am proud to be the first American president to visit Ireland during his term of office, proud to be addressing this distinguished assembly, and proud of the welcome you have given me. My presence and your welcome, however, only symbolize the many and the enduring links which have bound the Irish and the Americans since the earliest days.

Benjamin Franklin, the envoy of the American Revolution, who was also born in Boston, was received by the Irish Parliament in 1772. It was neither independent nor free from discrimination at the time, but Franklin reported its members 'disposed to be friends of America'. 'By joining our interest with theirs,' he said, 'a more equitable treatment ... might be obtained for both nations.'

'Our two nations, divided by distance, have been united by history.'

Our interests have been joined ever since. Franklin sent leaflets to Irish freedom fighters. O'Connell was influenced by Washington, and Emmet influenced Lincoln. Irish volunteers played so predominant a role in the American Army that Lord Mountjoy lamented in the British Parliament, 'We have lost America through the Irish.' John Barry, whose statue was honoured yesterday, and whose sword is in my office, was only one who fought for liberty in America to set an example for liberty in Ireland. Yesterday was the 117th anniversary of the birth of Charles Stewart Parnell – whose grandfather fought under Barry and whose mother was born in America – who, at the age of 34, was invited to address the American Congress on the cause of Irish freedom. 'I have seen since I have been in this country,' he said, 'so many tokens of the good wishes of the American people toward Ireland ... ' And today, 83 years later, I can say to you that I have seen in this country so many tokens of good wishes of the Irish people toward America.

And so it is that our two nations, divided by distance, have been united by history. No people ever believed more deeply in the cause of Irish freedom than the people of the United States. And no country contributed more to building my own than your sons and daughters. They came to our shores in a mixture of hope and agony, and I would not underrate the difficulties of their course once they arrived in the United States. They left behind hearts, fields and a nation yearning to be free. It is no wonder that James Joyce described the Atlantic as a bowl of bitter tears, and an earlier poet wrote, 'They are going, going, going and we cannot bid them stay.'

But today this is no longer the country of hunger and famine that those immigrants left behind. It is not rich and its progress is not yet complete, but it is, according to statistics, one of the best-fed countries in the world. Nor is it any longer a country of persecution, political or religious. It is a free country, and that is why any American feels at home.

There are those who regard this history of past strife and exile as better forgotten, but to use the phrase of Yeats, 'Let us not casually reduce that great past to a trouble of fools, for we need not feel the bitterness of the past to discover its meaning for the present and the future.'

'In the years since independence, you have undergone a new and peaceful revolution.'

And it is the present and the future of Ireland that today hold so much promise to my nation as well as to yours, and, indeed, to all mankind, for the Ireland of 1963, one of the youngest of nations, and the oldest of civilizations, has discovered that the achievement of nationhood is not an end, but a beginning. In the years since independence, you have undergone a new and peaceful revolution, an economic and industrial revolution, transforming the face of this land, while still holding to the old spiritual and cultural values. You have modernized your economy, harnessed your rivers, diversified your industry, liberalized your trade, electrified your farms, accelerated your rate of growth, and improved the living standard of your people.

Other nations of the world in whom Ireland has long invested her people and her children are now investing their capital as well as their vacations here in Ireland. This revolution is not yet over, nor will it be, I am sure, until a fully modern Irish economy fully shares in world prosperity. But prosperity is not enough.

One hundred and eighty-three years ago, Henry Grattan, demanding the more independent Irish Parliament that would always bear his name, denounced those who were satisfied merely by new grants of economic opportunity. 'A country,' he said, 'enlightened as Ireland, chartered as Ireland, armed as Ireland, and injured as Ireland, will not be satisfied with anything less than liberty.' And today, I am certain, free Ireland, a full fledged member of the world community, where some are not yet free, and where some counsel an acceptance of tyranny – free Ireland will not be satisfied with anything less than liberty.

I am glad, therefore, that Ireland is moving in the mainstream of current world events. For I sincerely believe that your future is as promising as your past is proud, and that your destiny lies not as a peaceful island in a sea of troubles, but as a maker and shaper of world peace … Ireland has already set an example and a standard for other small nations to follow. This has never been a rich or powerful country, and, yet, since earliest times, its influence on the world has been rich and powerful. No larger nation did more to keep Christianity and Western culture alive in their darkest centuries. No larger nation did more to spark the cause of American independence, and independence, indeed, around the world. And no larger nation has ever provided the world with more literary and artistic genius.

'It is that quality of the Irish, the remarkable combination of hope, confidence and imagination, that is needed more than ever today.'

This is an extraordinary country. George Bernard Shaw, speaking as an Irishman, summed up an approach to life, 'Other people,' he said, 'see things and say, "Why?" … But I dream things that never were – and I say, "Why not?"' It is that quality of the Irish, the remarkable combination of hope, confidence and imagination, that is needed more than ever today. The problems of the world cannot possibly be solved by sceptics or cynics whose horizons are limited by the obvious realities. We need men who can dream of things that never were, and ask why not. It matters not how small a nation is that seeks world peace and freedom, for, to paraphrase a citizen of my country, 'The humblest nation of all the world, when clad in the armour of a righteous cause, is stronger than all the hosts of error.'

Ireland is clad in the cause of national and human liberty with peace. To the extent that the peace is disturbed by conflict between the former colonial powers and the new and developing nations, Ireland's role is unique. For every new nation knows that Ireland was the first of the small nations in the 20th century to win its struggle for independence, and that the Irish have traditionally sent their doctors and technicians and soldiers and priests to help other lands to keep their liberty alive …

'Like the Irish missionaries of medieval days … you are not content to sit by your fireside.'

The major forum for your nation's greater role in world affairs is that of protector of the weak and voice of the small, the United Nations. From Cork to the Congo, from Galway to the Gaza Strip, from this legislative assembly to the United Nations, Ireland is sending its most talented men to do the world's most important work – the work of peace. In a sense, this export of talent is in keeping with an historic Irish role. But you no longer go as exiles and emigrants but for the service of your country and, indeed, of all men. Like the Irish missionaries of medieval days, like the Wild Geese after the Battle of the Boyne, you are not content to sit by your fireside while others are in need of your help. Nor are you content with the recollections of the past when you face the responsibilities of the present …

'Ireland's hour has come. You have something to give to the world, and that is a future of peace with freedom.'

Great powers have their responsibilities and their burdens, but the smaller nations of the world must fulfil their obligations as well. A great Irish poet once wrote, 'I believe profoundly in the future of Ireland, that this is an isle of destiny, that that destiny will be glorious, and that when our hour has come we will have something to give to the world.'

My friends, Ireland's hour has come. You have something to give to the world, and that is a future of peace with freedom. Thank you.

'The seventies will be socialist.'

Brendan Corish
(1918–90)

Speech to the Labour Party Annual Conference, Dublin, 13 October 1967

'The seventies will be socialist,' proclaimed Labour leader Brendan Corish to the 1967 party conference. This seemed a bizarre, even crazy, boast. Ireland, unlike most of its western European counterparts, had no effective left-wing movement. The hostility of the Catholic church had seen communism and socialism stigmatized as dirty words. Yet Corish believed that national and international developments might herald a new red dawn. The direct influence of the church had begun to moderate. All the Irish parties were committed to economic planning and had even begun to portray themselves as left-wing. Seán Lemass had announced that Fianna Fáil was taking a swing to the left; Fine Gael was promoting a 'just society'. Fearing that other parties were stealing its clothes, Labour looked around for new ways to re-establish its radical credentials. In the end the party decided to embrace the socialist tradition.

Corish's speech in October 1967 was a fine piece of rhetoric that was both critical and inspiring. It came a year after the Easter Rising jubilee celebrations, when many had questioned if independent Ireland had lived up to the goals of 1916. Corish argued that cynicism and indifference were prevalent in Irish society and that young people wanted a new approach. This was an appeal to youth that reflected the rhetoric of John F. Kennedy and (more prosaically) Harold Wilson. The speech, drafted by two *Irish Times* journalists, was expertly written and passionately delivered. Even opponents widely regarded it as a *tour de force*.

Yet a superb speech could not achieve the impossible for Ireland. The seventies produced Dana, flares and platform shoes but little socialism.

BIOGRAPHY

Brendan Corish was born in 1918 in Wexford, from where his father would be elected to Dáil Éireann in 1921. Brendan 'inherited' the seat in 1945 and was returned at every subsequent general election he fought. He was minister for social welfare in 1954–7. Given his reputation as a bishops' man, many were surprised that as Labour leader from 1960 he pushed the party to the left to embrace socialism. He took Labour into government in 1973–7, serving as tánaiste and minister for health in the Cosgrave national coalition government. Corish retired from politics at the 1982 general election and died eight years later in Wexford.

The seventies will be socialist. At the next general election Labour must for the third successive time make a major breakthrough in seats and votes. It must demonstrate convincingly that it has the capacity to become the government of this country.

The Labour Party can only achieve its objectives by attaining the power of government. Our present position is a mere transition phase on the road to securing the support of the majority of our people. At the next general election (the most crucial in our history) it must face the electorate with a clear-cut alternative to the conservatism of the past and present; and emerge from the election as the party which will shape the seventies.

What I offer now is the outline of a new society, a new republic ...

As a people we face a crisis of decision. We have never seriously made a choice of the type of society we wished to build here. We took one over without question, and have attempted to make it work, but without success.

'Do we accept man's basic dignity as the starting point of all government policy?'

It is necessary now to engage in deep questioning – to question what is the purpose of politics, what is the purpose of society. Are individuals to fend for themselves, each in a spirit of competitive hostility, or are we to work together so that equality and freedom may allow each man to develop as he sees fit? Do we accept man's basic dignity as the starting point of all government policy?

As a socialist party we accept that as our starting point. In economics the purpose of our national plan will be to achieve a thriving economy; in the social services, our purpose will be to provide a high level of welfare.

Socialism is a real alternative. It puts forward the concept of a new society in contrast to the one we now have. Our purpose in politics is to see to it that the question is put, and that the decision is made.

There is urgency in our approach to the national problems because we want them to be tackled now before they go beyond the point where it would be impossible.

'Socialism is a real alternative.'

We put it clearly. In our circumstances there is no alternative to socialism.

In saying that the new republic must be socialist, Labour is not merely invoking a magic word that will dispel all evil simply by being uttered. Labour believes, with Connolly, that socialism is not a set of settled doctrines to be applied dogmatically to every situation but essentially is an attitude capable of being developed in many ways. It is, as one writer has said, a set of moral attitudes, a belief in fraternal co-operation rather than the competitive hostility of capitalism ...

The Irish Labour Party today may be less sophisticated, less powerful than its counterpart in other countries. But we are heirs to a tradition of brave struggle. The

Defenders in the 18th century preceded the '98 Rising in their violent defence of working-class rights. Tone drew his strength from 'the men of no property', and Fenianism was strongest in the areas where the workers had made the strongest fights. 1913, that magnificent demonstration of working-class solidarity, set the mood for 1916.

All of us know that Irish Labour has disappointed even its most fervent supporters. Perhaps some of the reasons for this can be found in an examination of the elements which make up our movement. The trade unions up to now have not played the role they should have in projecting socialist policies, the role that Connolly and Larkin advocated. In rural areas, our supporters have tended to be too easily satisfied with partial success. The young radicals in our cities, until recently, have criticized from outside our ranks. The party, too, has been a victim of the cynicism which followed the failure of the political parties to establish the republic of equality envisaged by Connolly and Pearse.

'Labour has disappointed even its most fervent supporters.'

Strong criticism is good for this party. It is right that we should be reminded of our faults and shortcomings. Some of us may disagree. We have every right to do so; this is a party of dissent and the debate should reach out to every issue which affects our community. Harsh words will be said and accepted. This is not a rigid party. No section of it has a monopoly of patriotism. And the continued repetition of the same statements, night after night, no matter from what hallowed source, is not often the best way of influencing comrades. Neither is criticism enough. Constructive and realistic alternatives to the present conservative policies are essential.

I am convinced that from this full and free debate will develop a vital Labour movement in this island – a movement to which we all can give deep loyalty.

I am convinced that the people will accept this alternative of the new republic. We have embarked on a noble adventure which no Irishman who feels deeply about his country can ignore.

Comrades, let us go forward together.

'*Ulster stands at the crossroads.*'

Terence O'Neill
(1914–90)

National television broadcast, 9 December 1968

The Northern Ireland 'troubles' began in the television age, which meant they played out nightly in people's living rooms. As the province spun out of control, so all sides increasingly looked to advance their cause by taking advantage of the new medium. The Northern Ireland Civil Rights Association took its cue from the US civil rights movement in adopting the televisually powerful tactic of protest marching. Loyalists, for whom parading was such a part of their culture that it had its own season, interpreted this move as highly provocative.

The first major civil rights march took place at Dungannon on 24 August 1968 and set a pattern of demonstration and counter-demonstration. Unlike subsequent marches, this initial one passed off peacefully. The first gathering to attract serious violence took place in Derry on 5 October 1968. Banned by the Stormont government, the march only numbered a few hundred, but the RUC's reaction lent the occasion an importance that far outweighed the turnout. Officers used water cannon on the crowds and baton-charged the protestors. Fifty people were hospitalized. Images broadcast that night of police attacks, notably one on Belfast MP Gerry Fitt, prompted widespread anger in both communities and drew global condemnation.

The public nature of the violence prompted intervention from London. In November, Northern Ireland's prime minister, Terence O'Neill, was summoned to see British premier Harold Wilson. There he was presented with a package of reform based on the demands of the civil rights movement. This included root and branch change in local government, including housing provision and 'one man, one vote' local elections. The reforms went too far for extreme loyalist opinion. Even members of O'Neill's government publicly expressed anger at the proposals. O'Neill, looking tired and a little desperate, gambled on 9 December by using television to appeal over the heads of critics to moderate opinion. It was a risk that paid off in the short term. Most of his party, the media, the clergy and public opinion were vociferous in their support (which included 150,000 letters of encouragement). Bolstered by this sense of goodwill, O'Neill dramatically and symbolically sacked William Craig, the home affairs minister and his most vocal opponent in cabinet.

BIOGRAPHY

Terence O'Neill was born at Hyde Park in London in 1914, the son of a Unionist MP, Arthur O'Neill, the first MP to be killed during the First World War. Educated at Eton, he eschewed university to serve in the Irish Guards during the Second World War. Elected to Stormont in 1946, O'Neill succeeded Viscount Brookeborough as Unionist leader and prime minister of Northern Ireland in 1963. He became the first Northern Ireland premier to greet his counterpart from Dublin when he met Seán Lemass in 1965. Following his resignation in 1969, he took a keen interest in his Irish lineage. He died at his home, Lisle Court, on 12 June 1990.

O'Neill's plea to step back from the brink was heeded by moderate civil rights demonstrators. But radical activists such as People's Democracy sought to increase tension rather than let things settle down. They organized a march from Belfast to Derry, setting out on New Year's Day 1969. As they neared Derry on 4 January, loyalist extremists, including off-duty members of the Ulster Special Constabulary, ambushed them at Burntollet bridge.

If Ulster had been 'at the crossroads', the attack at Burntollet confirmed which direction the province was heading. Terence O'Neill resigned soon afterwards, a broken man.

Ulster stands at the crossroads. I believe you know me well enough by now to appreciate that I am not a man given to extravagant language. But I must say to you this evening that our conduct over the coming days and weeks will decide our future …

'I ask you now with all sincerity to call your people off the streets.'

And now I want to say a word directly to those who have been demonstrating for civil rights. The changes which we have announced are genuine and far-reaching changes and the government as a whole is committed to them. I would not continue to preside over an administration which would water them down or make them meaningless. You will see when the members of the Londonderry Commission are appointed that we intend to live up to our words that this will be a body to command confidence and respect. You will see that in housing allocations we mean business. You will see that legislation to appoint an ombudsman will be swiftly introduced. Perhaps you are not entirely satisfied: but this is a democracy and I ask you now with all sincerity to call your people off the streets and allow an atmosphere of change to develop. You are Ulstermen yourselves. You know we are all of us stubborn people who will not be pushed too far. I believe that most of you want change, not revolution. Your voice has been heard, and clearly heard. Your duty now is to play your part in taking the heat out of the situation before blood is shed.

But I have a word too, for all those others who see in change a threat to our position in the United Kingdom. I say to them, unionism, armed with justice, will be a stronger cause than unionism armed merely with strength. The bully-boy tactics we saw in Armagh are no answer to these grave problems: but they incur for us the contempt of Britain and the world. And such contempt is the greatest threat to Ulster. Let the government govern and the police take care of law and order.

What, in any case, are these changes which we have decided must come? They all amount to this: that in every aspect of our life justice must not only be done but be seen to be done to all sections of the community. There must be evident fairness as between one man and another.

'What kind of Ulster do you want?'

The adoption of such reforms will not, I believe, lose a single seat for those who support the unionist cause and, indeed, some may be gained. And remember that it is with Stormont that the power of decision rests for maintaining our constitution.

And now a further word to you all. What kind of Ulster do you want? A happy and respected province in good standing with the rest of the United Kingdom? Or a place continually torn apart by riots and demonstrations and regarded by the rest of Britain as a political outcast? As always, in a democracy, the choice is yours. I will accept whatever your verdict may be. If it is your decision that we should live up to the words 'Ulster is British', which is part of our creed, then my services will be at your disposal to do what I can. But if you should want a separate inward-looking, selfish and divided Ulster, then you must seek for others to lead you along that road for I cannot and will not do it. Please weigh well all that is at stake and make your voice heard in whatever way you think best so that we may know the views not of the few, but of the many. For this is truly a time of decision and in your silence all that we have built up could be lost. I pray that you will reflect carefully and decide wisely. And I ask all our Christian people, whatever their denomination, to attend their places of worship on Sunday next to pray for the peace and harmony of our country.

'There is no place in society for us.'

Bernadette Devlin

(b.1947)

Speech to the House of Commons, Westminster, 22 April 1969

Bernadette Devlin was a psychology undergraduate at Queen's University, Belfast, when she became involved in People's Democracy, a student-led, socialist republican group founded in 1968. The organization was more militant than the Northern Ireland Civil Rights Association that preceded it, and Devlin, alongside fellow Queen's students Michael Farrell and Eamon McCann, became one of its best-known faces.

Following the death of George Forrest, Unionist MP for mid-Ulster, Devlin was chosen to contest the by-election as an independent unity candidate at Westminster running against Forrest's widow. Devlin won the seat to become, aged 21, the youngest woman ever elected to the House of Commons.

The custom at Westminster was for new MPs to devote their maiden speeches to uncontentious subjects. On her election, however, Devlin had promised, 'When I get to Westminster, I am going to shout that the peasants have come into their own.' It is scarcely surprising that her maiden speech on 22 April 1969 was much anticipated. One reporter noted that the chamber was packed, 'the peers' benches ... a solid mass of aristocracy [and] the foreign press gallery overflowing'. Despite her reputation as an uncompromising campaigner for civil rights in Northern Ireland, Devlin's youth and gender ensured that the media portrayed her with a combination of paternalism and condescension. Describing her entrance to the floor of the Commons, *The Times* described her as 'a Lilliputian and apparently timid little figure' (at five feet tall), remarking that her spirit 'bore little relationship to her size. She is a bonny fighter, and from the start of her 25-minute harangue she had the House enthralled.'

BIOGRAPHY

Bernadette Devlin was born in 1947 in Cookstown, County Tyrone, to a Catholic family. Educated at St Patrick's Girls' Academy and at Queen's University, Belfast, she was elected MP for mid-Ulster at a by-election in 1969. Devlin lost that seat in 1974 and has not held elected office since. Active in establishing the Irish Republican Socialist Party, the political wing of the Irish National Liberation Army (INLA), in 1974, she resigned from the movement the following year and later joined the Independent Socialist Party, which disbanded shortly afterwards. She was a vocal supporter of the hunger strikers in 1980–1. In 1982 she twice ran unsuccessfully for Dáil Éireann.

Three years later, in the aftermath of 'Bloody Sunday' (when 13 Catholic civil rights marchers were shot dead in Derry by paratroopers), Devlin achieved infamy at Westminster by physically attacking the home secretary, Reginald Maudling, whom she called a 'murdering hypocrite'. *The Times* reported that such an attack on a minister 'was without parallel'. Devlin was suspended from the House of Commons for six months. She lost her seat at the 1974 general election.

'There is no place in society for us.'

‘I understand that in making my maiden speech on the day of my arrival in Parliament and in making it on a controversial issue I flaunt the unwritten traditions of the House, but I think that the situation of my people merits the flaunting of such traditions.

As the hon. Member for Londonderry [Mr Chichester Clark] rightly said, there never was born an Englishman who understands the Irish people. Thus a man who is alien to the ordinary working Irish people cannot understand them, and I therefore respectfully suggest that the hon. gentleman has no understanding of my people, because Catholics and Protestants are the ordinary people, the oppressed people from whom I come and whom I represent. I stand here as the youngest woman in Parliament in the same tradition as the first woman ever to be elected to this Parliament, Constance Markievicz, who was elected on behalf of the Irish people …

'There never was born an Englishman who understands the Irish people.'

The hon. Member for Londonderry said that he stood in Bogside. I wonder whether he could name the streets through which he walked in the Bogside so that we might establish just how well acquainted he became with the area. I had never hoped to see the day when I might agree with someone who represents the bigoted and sectarian Unionist Party, which uses a deliberate policy of dividing the people in order to keep the ruling minority in power and to keep the oppressed people of Ulster oppressed. I never thought I could see the day when I should agree with any phrase uttered by the representative of such a party, but the hon. gentleman summed up the situation 'to a t'. He referred to stark, human misery. That is what I saw in Bogside. It has been there for 50 years – and that same stark human misery is to be found in the Protestant Fountain area, which the hon. gentleman would claim to represent.

These are the people the hon. gentleman would claim to want to join society. Because they are equally poverty stricken they are equally excluded from the society which the Unionist Party represents as the society of landlords who, by ancient charter of Charles II, still hold the right of the ordinary people of Northern Ireland over such things as fishing and as paying the most ridiculous and exorbitant rents, although families have lived for generations on their land. But this is the ruling minority of landlords who, for generations, have claimed to represent one section of the people and, in order to maintain their claim, divide the people into two sections and stand up in this House to say that there are those who do not wish to join society.

'There is no place in society for us, the ordinary 'peasants' of Northern Ireland.'

The people in my country who do not wish to join the society which is represented by the hon. Member for Londonderry are by far the majority. There is no place in society for us, the ordinary 'peasants' of Northern Ireland. There is no place for us in the society of landlords because we are the 'have-nots' and they are the 'haves'.

We came to the situation in Derry when the people had had enough. Since 5 October, it has been the unashamed and deliberate policy of the Unionist government to try to force an image on the civil rights movement that it was nothing more than a Catholic uprising. The people in the movement have struggled desperately to overcome that image, but it is impossible when the ruling minority are the government and control not only political matters but the so-called impartial forces of law and order. It is impossible then for us to state quite fairly where we stand.

How can we say that we are a non-sectarian movement and are for the rights of both Catholics and Protestants when, clearly, we are beaten into the Catholic areas? Never have we been beaten into the Protestant areas. When the students marched from Belfast to Derry, there was a predominant number of Protestants. The number of non-Catholics was greater than the number of Catholics. Nevertheless, we were still beaten into the Catholic area because it was in the interests of the minority and the Unionist Party to establish that we were nothing more than the Catholic uprising ...

'The Irish government can no longer stand by.'

Jack Lynch
(1917–99)

Broadcast on RTÉ television, 13 August 1969

The summer of 1969 had seen serious rioting in Northern Ireland, but it was not until the tail end of the 'marching season' that violence escalated to a deadly scale. Derry had been the site of violent confrontation at marches on several occasions. When the loyalist perpetrators of Burntollet returned to Derry afterwards, they had been met with a hero's welcome. Riots and attacks on Catholic homes in the Bogside followed. This prompted the erection of barricades around the area and the establishment of 'Free Derry', a no-go area for the security forces. On 12 August, an Apprentice Boys parade with Royal Ulster Constabulary (RUC) protection came under attack from a hail of stones thrown by Catholic youths. The police chased the stone-throwers back to the Bogside, which had defences ready for such an eventuality. Thus began a siege that lasted 3 days and saw 112 people hospitalized. The city had descended into a state of anarchy.

Reaction in the Republic to images of RUC violence was one of outrage. The taoiseach, Jack Lynch, appeared on television on 13 August to express the government's concern at the situation and to announce that the Irish army would set up field hospitals along the border to look after Catholic refugees.

Lynch had outlined limited measures to assist those affected by violence, but much more was read into his assertion that the Republic 'can no longer stand by'. Interpreted by Protestants as a threat, the words provoked violence in Belfast. This reached its nadir when loyalist mobs sacked Catholic Bombay Street. Seven people died and thousands of families were displaced. The day after Lynch's speech, the British Army in the shape of the Prince of Wales's Regiment arrived in Derry to relieve the siege. Catholics welcomed them with open arms.

The honeymoon was shortlived: the relationship between northern Catholics and the British Army quickly disintegrated, adding yet another problem to an already nightmarish state of affairs.

BIOGRAPHY

Jack Lynch was born in Cork in 1917 and educated by the Christian Brothers and at University College, Cork. An outstanding athlete, he won a record six successive All-Ireland medals for Cork (five in hurling, one in football). Elected to Dáil Éireann in 1948, he succeeded Seán Lemass as Fianna Fáil leader in 1966, serving as taoiseach in 1966–73 and 1977–9. Famously, Lynch presided over the Arms Crisis of 1970, during which he was viewed as a force for constitutional stability. He resigned mid-term in 1979 and retired from politics at the next general election in 1981. Lynch died in Dublin on 20 October 1999 and was buried at St Finbarr's Cemetery in his native Cork. He remains among Ireland's most affectionately remembered leaders.

It is with deep sadness that you, Irish men and women of goodwill, and I have learned of the tragic events which have been taking place in Derry and elsewhere in the North in recent days. Irishmen in every part of this island have made known their concern at these events. This concern is heightened by the realization that the spirit of reform and inter-communal co-operation has given way to the forces of sectarianism and prejudice. All people of goodwill must feel saddened and disappointed at this backward turn in events and must be apprehensive for the future.

'We deplore sectarianism and intolerance.'

The government fully share these feelings and I wish to repeat that we deplore sectarianism and intolerance in all their forms wherever they occur. The government have been very patient and have acted with great restraint over several months past. While we made our views known to the British government on a number of occasions, both by direct contact and through our diplomatic representatives in London, we were careful to do nothing that would exacerbate the situation. But it is clear now that the present situation cannot be allowed to continue.

'The Irish government can no longer stand by and see innocent people injured and perhaps worse.'

It is evident, also, that the Stormont government is no longer in control of the situation. Indeed the present situation is the inevitable outcome of the policies pursued for decades by successive Stormont governments. It is clear, also, that the Irish government can no longer stand by and see innocent people injured and perhaps worse.

It is obvious that the RUC is no longer accepted as an impartial police force. Neither would the employment of British troops be acceptable nor would they be likely to restore peaceful conditions, certainly not in the long term. The Irish government have, therefore, requested the British government to apply immediately to the United Nations for the urgent dispatch of a peace-keeping force to the six counties of Northern Ireland and have instructed the Irish permanent representative to the United Nations to inform the secretary-general of this request. We have also asked the British government to see to it that police attacks on the people of Derry should cease immediately.

Very many people have been injured and some of them seriously. We know that many of these do not wish to be treated in six-county hospitals. We have, therefore, directed the Irish Army authorities to have field hospitals established in County

Donegal adjacent to Derry and at other points along the border where they may be necessary.

Recognizing, however, that the reunification of the national territory can provide the only permanent solution for the problem, it is our intention to request the British government to enter into early negotiations with the Irish government to review the present constitutional position of the six counties of Northern Ireland.

'Reunification of the national territory can provide the only permanent solution.'

These measures which I have outlined to you seem to the government to be those most immediately and urgently necessary.

All men and women of goodwill will hope and pray that the present deplorable and distressing situation will not further deteriorate but that it will soon be ended firstly by the granting of full equality of citizenship to every man and woman in the six-county area regardless of class, creed or political persuasion and, eventually, by the restoration of the historic unity of our country.

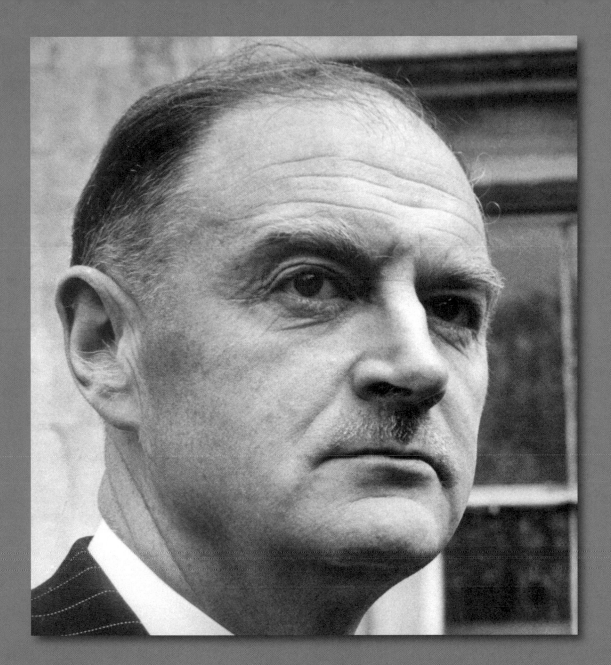

'Mongrel foxes.'

Liam Cosgrave
(b.1920)

Speech at Cork City Hall, 21 May 1972

By the time the Fine Gael Ard Fheis (party conference) met in May 1972, the party had come through a particularly frustrating period. Fianna Fáil had been in office for an uninterrupted 15 years, helped at the 1969 election by Labour's go-it-alone policy, which ruled out an anti-Fianna Fáil coalition with Fine Gael. Even the arms crisis of 1970, when Charles Haughey and Neil Blaney were dismissed from office and later charged with conspiracy to import arms, failed to dislodge the government. The one positive development for Fine Gael was the decision by Labour to abandon its anti-coalition policy. The down side for Fine Gael was the distasteful prospect of co-operation with Labour's many left-wing radicals. These elements had been out in force a week earlier unsuccessfully campaigning for a 'no' vote in the referendum on whether Ireland should join the EEC.

By the time the conference met, the Fine Gael leader, Liam Cosgrave, was furious with everyone. The government, the Labour Party and republican groups were all in his sights. But caught right in the crosshairs of Cosgrave's indignation were liberal elements in his own party. Cosgrave was firmly on the traditional wing of Fine Gael. He had broadly supported the reformist ideas of Declan Costello and the 'Just Society', but in the context of the arms crisis, his primary concern was defending the institutions of the state. A mixture of ideological frustration and personal ambition had prompted a group of 'young tigers' – particularly the deputy leader T.F. O'Higgins and the newly elected deputy Garret FitzGerald – to plot ceaselessly to oust him as party leader. Cosgrave was predictably angered at this disloyalty, not least because it came at the time of national emergency.

The year 1972 was the 50th anniversary of the founding of the state. This was all but ignored by the government, yet it was an anniversary that had a special resonance for Fine Gael generally, and for Cosgrave in particular. His father, W.T. Cosgrave, had succeeded Griffith and Collins as president of the executive council. When Cosgrave came to address the 4000 delegates gathered in Cork City Hall, he delivered a forceful enunciation of Fine Gael's commitment to democracy and security. This had been expected, but few, if any, had an inkling of what

BIOGRAPHY

Liam Cosgrave was born in Dublin in 1920, the son of W.T. Cosgrave, the first head of government of the Irish Free State. Educated at Castleknock College and King's Inns, he was elected to Dáil Éireann in 1943, aged just 23, and sat alongside his father. Parliamentary secretary to the taoiseach (1948–51), he was minister for external affairs (1954–7). Cosgrave succeeded James Dillon as leader of Fine Gael in 1965, serving as taoiseach of the national coalition government in 1973–7. He resigned as party leader after losing the 1977 election and retired from politics in 1981. His son, also Liam, was elected that same year, but lost his seat in 1987. This ended an unbroken run of Cosgrave representation in Dáil Éireann that stretched back to 1918.

'Mongrel foxes.'

would come next. Cosgrave finished by departing from his script to threaten his rivals in the party. Until now, he had remained silent on the issue in public, but his allusion to the young tigers as 'mongrel foxes', and his promise to 'dig them out' was both shocking and brutal.

This culture war would continue into government in 1973–7, most strikingly when efforts to liberalize contraceptive provision collapsed in acrimony as Liam Cosgrave, now taoiseach, voted against his own Fine Gael/Labour administration.

This year it is right that we should recall the 50th anniversary not only of the establishment of the institutions of state and the part played in that historic achievement by Griffith and Collins, but is also right that we should direct our minds and energies to the future … In getting where we are, we had to withstand abuse and vilification, setbacks and disappointments but our courage and faith in the democratic forces enabled us to survive and grow to our present numbers. Fortified by this strength we face the future with faith in ourselves and the people.

The recent decision by the people in the … [European Economic Community] referendum has been rightly interpreted as a mass demonstration by the great majority of the Irish people that they desire peace and progress, and especially that they do not want anarchists or agitators stirring up riots and civil disorders with the object of overthrowing the lawfully established authority of the state. As long as the present violence continues in the North there can be no complacency about security in the Republic. The danger to democratic government in the Republic presented by the activities of unlawful organizations has been and still is very real. The vigilance of the Army and Gardaí has been a major factor in maintaining the security of the state during the past two or three years.

It is with pride we recall that the Army and our unarmed police force were the creations of Collins and Griffith and those who served with them in the first government of the state. During the 50 years of native government since 1922 the men of the Army and the Gardaí have continued to uphold the authority of the Irish Parliament and of the rule of law. We, the people whom they serve, owe them unstinting support and gratitude for that protection.

It certainly cannot be said that the present government has at any time been sufficiently committed to the work of stamping out unlawful military or para-military organizations. These groups and their leaders, as I have repeatedly pointed out, have no mandate for their policies of violence and disruption, and have never had to face an Irish electorate. Yet they have been allowed to call public meetings and news conferences, and to hold demonstrations, in which they have openly advocated unlawful military action and the subversion of lawful authority.

How long more is the present intolerable situation to continue, in which the government is incapable of effectively dealing with illegal and irregular groups because of its own internal party problems? In the present serious political and economic situation the government is dependent on support from certain FF deputies who are in conflict with the alleged government policy on these matters, but who do not vote against the government. On the other hand, the government ostensibly rejects the attitude of these deputies, but is prepared to retain office and place and power through their support. This attitude shows the duplicity of FF and in present circumstances its reckless disregard for action not only in the letter, but in the spirit of recognized democratic standards.

'How long more is the present intolerable situation to continue?'

This attitude has resulted in a wide range of national problems being either ignored or mishandled, for example, the grave problem of unemployment. The government and FF Party are so preoccupied in settling their internal conflicts, with trimming statements to satisfy the verbal patriotism of some of their supporters in the Dáil, that the welfare of the people takes second place.

The task of uniting Ireland is the remaining over-riding national political problem. It will require statesmanship, courage, patience and determination to achieve this objective. Some alien, indeed Communist, influences are at work in trying to set Irishman against Irishman. Catholic against Protestant. These same elements tried their hands unsuccessfully in the Referendum. They assumed the spurious mantle of adopted patriotism to disguise their real intentions. This party never refused, nor was it ever afraid to expose such activities, and to condemn similar anti-Irish activities as against the people's interest.

'The time has now arrived to make a fresh start.'

Anarchy must be resisted; it cannot help any section, religious or political and those who would suffer most would be the weak, the old and the poor. The time has now arrived to make a fresh start on reuniting all the people of Ireland … We have consistently stated our basic conviction that the problem of the division of Ireland can only be solved by agreement; but much more is required than a repudiation of violence. There must be from this part of the country a positive sustained programme designed to eliminate suspicion and erase misunderstandings. This can best be done at the practical level of identifying joint interests and areas in which people from every part of the country can work together …

The service this party can render at present to the Irish people is to urge with all our strength the importance, because of the gravity of the situation, of immediate talks between Ireland and Britain in consultation with the elected representatives in the North of Ireland for the purpose of seeking a permanent settlement of that problem. There will be no lasting peace in the North of Ireland until Ireland is reunited. This should be faced now, and lives saved as a result. This will involve guaranteeing fundamental religious, political and civil rights for Catholics and Protestants, it will involve over a period guarantees by the Irish and British governments and a financial contribution from Britain – it is better for Britain to incur a short-term financial liability than a continuous drain of a heavier type. Unless we are prepared as a nation to travel this road there can be no peace based on justice. Let the party then, lead the nation on the right road to peace in Ireland.

(He then departed from his speech.)

The party now faces what might be the most critical stage in its history. Some members of the party have given their time to building it up when they might have been better occupied to their own advantage. They have made it possible for members to come into the organization and squeak and bleat about something which they knew themselves they could not achieve.

'Like mongrel foxes, they are gone to ground and I'll dig them out.'

I don't know whether some of you do any hunting or not, but some of these commentators and critics are now like mongrel foxes, they are gone to ground and I'll dig them out, and the pack will chop them when they get them.

'We are living away beyond
our means.'

Charles J. Haughey
(1925–2006)

Broadcast on RTÉ television, 9 January 1980

'We are living away beyond our means.'

Good as well as bad speeches can leave hostages to fortune. The well-crafted phrase or inspired soundbite can often come back to hoist speakers on their own verbal petard. This happened infamously to Charles J. Haughey following a television address on 9 January 1980.

Ireland had entered the 1980s with its economy in tatters. Mismanagement and inopportune pump-priming by successive governments, unrelenting wage inflation, a vast balance of payments deficit and years of global oil crises had crippled Ireland's economy. Matters had deteriorated rapidly since the 1977 general election when Fianna Fáil began implementing its 'jam for all' platform of tax cuts and greater public spending.

The result was meltdown. Interest rates rocketed. Unemployment reached a staggering 20 per cent. Almost 1.5 million days per annum were lost to industrial action. Several economists, characterized somewhat pejoratively as the 'Doheny and Nesbit [pub] school of economics' had long been demanding that fiscal rectitude should replace profligacy. It just needed someone to shout 'stop'.

That someone was Charles Haughey. Shortly after succeeding Jack Lynch as taoiseach, he appeared on television to declare the Irish were 'living away beyond our means'. It seemed to mark a new departure in a more responsible attitude towards public spending. This time round, Haughey's resolve proved shortlived; it was not long before the government shied away from proposed savage cutbacks. Vast numbers continued to fill social welfare offices or simply left the country. It was only Haughey's 1987–9 minority government that finally took spending and debt levels in hand.

Haughey's supporters, with some justification, credited him with laying the foundations of Ireland's 'economic miracle' of the 1990s. Yet even his friends found it hard to reconcile the fact that, while Haughey was telling the Irish people to tighten their belts, he himself was racking up a personal debt of more than a million pounds. The revelation that he had been using 'dig-outs' from businessmen to make good the shortfall

BIOGRAPHY

Charles J. Haughey was born in 1925 in Castlebar, County Mayo, and raised in Donnycarney, Dublin. He was educated at University College Dublin, and in 1951 married Maureen Lemass, the daughter of Seán Lemass. A member of the government from 1961, Jack Lynch sacked him as minister for finance in 1970 over the Arms Crisis, but then reappointed him to cabinet in 1977. Haughey succeeded Lynch as leader of Fianna Fáil in 1979, serving as taoiseach in 1979–81, 1982, 1987-9 and 1989–92. He resigned in 1992 after losing the confidence of Fianna Fáil's coalition partner, the Progressive Democrats, and some in his own party. Haughey left quoting Shakespeare, saying that he had 'done the state some service'. He died at Kinsealy in 2006 and was buried in St Fintan's Cemetery in Sutton after a state funeral.

made it difficult for them to counter the accusation that Haughey was at best a hypocrite and at worst a crook. That he was also among Ireland's most popular and seminal prime ministers only adds to a complicated legacy.

I wish to talk to you this evening about the state of the nation's affairs and the picture I have to paint is not, unfortunately, a very cheerful one.

'Our trading with the outside world in 1979 was bad.'

The figures which are just now becoming available to us show one thing very clearly. As a community we are living away beyond our means. I do not mean that everyone in the community is living too well. Clearly many are not and have barely enough to get by. But taking us all together, we have been living at a rate which is simply not justified by the amount of goods and services we are producing.

To make up the difference, we have been borrowing enormous amounts of money, borrowing at a rate which just cannot continue. A few simple figures will make this very clear.

At home, the government's current income from taxes and all other sources in 1979 fell short of what was needed to pay the running costs of the state by about £520 million. To meet this and our capital programme, we had to borrow in 1979 over £1000 million. That amount is equal to one-seventh of our entire national output for the year. This is just far too high a rate and cannot possibly continue.

The situation in regard to our trading with the outside world in 1979 was bad also. Our income from abroad fell short of what we had to pay out by about £760 million which led to a fall in our reserves.

'We must look not just on the home scene but also on the troubled and unstable world around us.'

To fully understand our situation, we must look not just on the home scene but also on the troubled and unstable world around us. There are wars and rumours of wars. There is political instability in some of the most important areas of the world. A very serious threat exists to the world's future supply of energy. We can no longer be sure that we will be able to go on paying the prices now being demanded for all the oil and other fuels we require to keep our factories going and to keep our homes and institutions supplied with the light, heat and power they need. We will, of course, push exploration for our own oil ahead as rapidly as possible but in the short term the burden of oil prices will continue to be a crushing one.

'We will have to continue to cut down on government spending.'

All this indicates that we must, first of all, as a matter of urgency, set about putting our domestic affairs in order and secondly, improving our trade with the rest of the world in so far as we can do so.

We will have to continue to cut down on government spending. The government is taking far too much by way of taxes from individual members of the community. But even this amount is not enough to meet our commitments. We will just have to reorganize government spending so that we can only undertake the things which we can afford.

In trying to bring government expenditure within manageable proportions, we will, of course, be paying particular attention to the needs of the poorer and weaker sections of the community and make sure they are looked after. Other essential community expenditure will have to be undertaken also. But there are many things which will just have to be curtailed or postponed, until such time as we can get the financial situation right.

There is one thing above all else which we can do to help get the situation right and which is entirely within our control. I refer to industrial relations. Any further serious interruption in production, or in the provision of essential services, in 1980 would be a major disaster. I believe that everyone listening to me tonight shares my anxiety about our situation in this respect.

'Let us clearly understand, however, that this is not a one-sided affair.'

Strikes, go-slows, work-to-rule, stoppages in key industries and essential services, were too often a feature of life in 1979. They caused suffering and hardship; at times it looked as if we were becoming one of those countries where basic services could not be relied upon to operate as part of normal life.

Immediately following my election as taoiseach, I received countless messages from all over the country from people in every walk of life, appealing to me to do something about this situation.

Let us clearly understand, however, that this is not a one-sided affair. Managements that do not give first-class attention to their firm's industrial relations, who ignore situations and let them drift into confrontation, are just as blameworthy as the handful of wild men who slap on an unofficial picket and stop thousands of workers from earning their living.

'What we need is a new way forward.'

Apportioning blame, however, is not going to get us anywhere. What we need is a new way forward and that is my primary purpose, as head of government, in talking to you tonight.

I am asking for a universal commitment to industrial peace in 1980. I am asking every worker and employer, every trade union, every employers' organization, every farmer and every farming organization, every housewife, in fact every individual citizen, to play a part in ending this humiliating, destructive industrial strife and putting in its place discussion, negotiations and peaceful settlements …

'People of Galway –
we love you!'

Joe Connolly
(b.1956)

Speech at Croke Park, Dublin, 7 September 1980

Joe Connolly captained the Galway team that beat Limerick 2–15 to 3–9 in the Senior Hurling All-Ireland final in 1980. This brought the Liam McCarthy Cup back to the county for the first time in almost 60 years. The infamous curse that had blighted Galway hurling for so long was finally broken. Folklore said that a local priest, having seen his parishioners leaving mass early to attend a hurling match in Dublin, swore an oath that the county would never again win an All-Ireland.

An exultant Connolly in accepting the cup delivered one of the most succinct and best-remembered speeches in the history of the Gaelic Athletic Association (GAA). Although most of the speech was given in beautiful Irish – Connolly was a native speaker – it was the last line, delivered in English, that caught the public imagination. He affectionately echoed not just the words but the accent and intonation of Pope John Paul II at a youth mass in the county the previous year. 'People of Galway,' Connolly proclaimed, 'We *love* you!'

Yet for all its wry humour, the speech contained a more poignant message. Connolly's words to emotional Galway exiles in England, in America and throughout the country stood as a reminder that millions had emigrated from the west of Ireland. The previous year's captain, Joe McDonagh, then gave a rousing rendition of 'The West's Awake'. In keeping with Connolly's use of the Pope's address, McDonagh, later president of the GAA, changed the words to 'when Galway lies in slumber deep'.

BIOGRAPHY

Joe Connolly was born in 1956 in Castlegar, County Galway. In 1980 he captained the Galway hurling team, which included his brother John, to their first All-Ireland title in more than half a century. That same year he won the All-Ireland senior club hurling championship with Castlegar and was named both Hurler of the Year and a Gaelic Athletic Association (GAA) All-Star. Connolly later became chairman of the GAA Alcohol and Substance Abuse Task Force and a director of the Irish-language television station TG4. 'I had nothing prepared,' said Connolly years later of his famous speech, 'because I thought after 57 years it would be tempting fate.'

The 1980 victory marked the first of a hat-trick of senior hurling championships for Galway that decade. Joe Connolly's victory address set the standard for winning captains and has been matched in recent times only by that of Cork's Seán Óg Ó hAilpín in 2005. ('His father from Fermanagh, his mother from Fiji – neither a hurling stronghold,' quipped Mícheál Ó Muircheartaigh).

In 2005 'People of Galway' was voted number eight in RTÉ television's Top GAA Moments.

A mhuintir na Gaillimhe, tar éis seacht mbliana agus caoga tá Craobh na hÉireann ar ais i nGaillimh. Is mór an onóir domsa mar chaptaen an corn seo a ghlacadh ar son an fhoireann uileag.

Is iontach an lá inniu le bheith mar Ghaillmheach. Tá daoine ar ais i nGaillimh agus tá gliondar ina gcroí. Ach freisin caithfimid cuimhneamh ar d[h]aoine i Sasana, i Meiriceá, ar fuaid na tíre. Agus tá siad, b'fhéidir, ag caoineadh anois i láthair.

(Ba mhaith liom freisin buíochas) a ghabháil do fhoireann Luimnigh as ucht an cluiche iontach a thug siad dúinn inniu. People of Galway – we love you!

Translation from Irish

People of Galway, after 57 years the all-Ireland [trophy] is back in Galway. It is a great honour for me as captain to accept this cup on behalf of all the team.

It is a wonderful day today to be from Galway. There are people back in Galway and there is joy in their hearts. But we also have to remember people in England, in America, throughout the country. And they are, perhaps, crying [with joy] at the moment.

(I would also like to thank) the Limerick team for the wonderful game they gave us today.

'Sit down and negotiate our future with us.'

John Hume
(b.1937)

Speech at Newcastle, County Down, 14 November 1981

The year 1981 was one of the most significant in the Northern Ireland 'troubles'. It had begun with the ongoing blanket and 'dirty' protests in the Maze Prison by IRA prisoners. They ultimately led to hunger strikes and the deaths of Bobby Sands and nine other hunger strikers. These had a huge impact on public opinion north and south, and in Britain, as they engendered extremes of sympathy and loathing.

The crisis had considerable political implications. H-Block candidates stood successfully for the Westminster and Dublin parliaments. Bobby Sands, the Provisional IRA's commander in the Maze, was elected MP for Fermanagh-South Tyrone in a by-election in April, less than a month before he died. At the general election in the Republic in June, nine H-block candidates stood, of whom two were elected. The level of support for the hunger strikers highlighted by street protests and by electoral success sent shockwaves through the political establishment in Dublin, Belfast and London. For republicans, it signalled the chance of political success without abandoning violence. As Sinn Féin's Danny Morrison famously put it, a united Ireland might be achieved with the 'ballot box in one hand and an armalite in the other'.

This left the Social Democratic and Labour Party (SDLP) tremendously exposed. Republicans were challenging the party for Catholic support in Northern Ireland. Their one ray of hope was the recent agreement between Margaret Thatcher and Garret FitzGerald to establish the Anglo-Irish Intergovernmental Council (AIIC). In addition, the British had promised that Dublin would have a say in the governance of Northern Ireland as part of a process of 'rolling devolution'. This horrified northern unionists. Tensions were heightened when the Reverend William Bradford, the Official Unionist MP for Belfast South, was shot dead by the Provisional IRA in November. Ian Paisley reacted by calling a unionist day of action and establishing a loyalist 'Third Force'.

It was in this volatile context that John Hume, leader of the SDLP since 1979, addressed the annual party conference on 14 November 1981. His speech was a direct plea for conciliation between moderate nationalists and unionists to prevent the extremes of republicanism and loyalism plunging Northern Ireland into the abyss.

BIOGRAPHY

John Hume was born in Derry in 1937 and became a founding member of the Social Democratic and Labour Party (SDLP) in August 1970. He took up the party leadership in 1979 after his predecessor, Gerry Fitt, had denounced the party as too nationalist in outlook. Elected MP for Foyle in 1983, Hume began exploratory talks with Gerry Adams in 1988 that helped pave the way for the peace process. Following the signing of the Belfast Agreement in 1998, he was awarded the Nobel Peace Prize jointly with David Trimble, before retiring from politics in 2004. 'John Hume and I were polls apart politically,' said Ian Paisley, 'but I liked him as a man.'

... I would say this to the Protestants of Northern Ireland: many among you can have little satisfaction in seeing the steady rise in the tyrannical dominance over you of a man whose name in every country in the world has become a byword for bigotry, demagoguery and obscurantism. Is Paisleyism in any sense consistent with those great Protestant values of individual freedom, free speech, civil and religious liberty of which you are so rightly proud? Is not what is being said and done in your name in Northern Ireland a gross and unworthy abuse of everything you stand for?

The essence of the appeal of unionism is that it is the only protection of Protestants in Ireland. Is it? Has it not instead seriously weakened your integrity and become a profound source politically and intellectually of real danger to the deepest values of the Protestant tradition in Ireland? Is it not time to consider that there are other ways, not only to protect the integrity of your tradition but to develop it and become a positive leaven in Irish society, challenging its uniformity? Is it not time to recognize that other ways do not involve conflict with your neighbours on this island but a fruitful partnership which recognizes the richness of difference and diversity? Surely not to consider other ways is to consign your own future, your children's future, our future, to despair, and surely you have no more right than we do to adopt such a nihilistic course. Must you – and now absurdly – permit your leaders to demand all power, exclusively and forever? For ourselves, we abjure any 'solution' in which there would be winners and losers, conquerors and vanquished, victory and defeat. So should you. Face reality with us and let us together be grateful that we have an opportunity to do so before catastrophe – which loomed over us earlier this year – overwhelms us all.

'We have to live together in the future.'

All we demand is that you and your leaders sit down and negotiate our future with us and the British and Irish governments. For our part, we would insist that the results of such talks would have to be ratified in two separate referenda, one in the North, the other in the South. That is a more secure guarantee of your rights than the cold and increasingly inconvenient device of the '73 Act. The principle of consent will be truly respected. We have to live together in the future. I know that many of you do not fully grasp my words. I know that you do not realize that when we say that we are proposing an 'Agreed Ireland' we mean those words absolutely literally. We mean an 'Agreed Ireland' which you would decisively help to shape. I ask you to reflect on our words because they do offer us the prospect of a future together within the limits of what is really possible ...

The nationalists of the North see in the Provisionals' activity the destruction of the integrity of their own political values, a direct attack on the real meaning of Irish unity. We also see in those parts of the community where the Provisional IRA are most active, the spread of a foul social cancer. The coherence of society at the best of times is both deep-rooted and fragile. Its roots, the shared principles of respect for life, liberty and order, can go deep but they must be tended and watered assiduously and incessantly. There are now communities in Northern Ireland where these roots have not alone been neglected, but have been hacked away and poisoned by the Provisional IRA's campaign against fundamental human rights to live until God calls us. What has followed is a gross distortion of moral values in society, the promotion of the pornography of death and nihilism on our gable walls and the deep corruption of the young. The SDLP will always recognize this evil for what it is and call it by its name: murder.

We say to the Provisionals you are not Irish republicans, you are extremists who have dishonoured and are dishonouring the deepest ideals of the Irish people. Can we remind you yet again that those whose inheritance you so falsely claim, laid down their arms in 1916 lest they cause any undue suffering to their Irish people.

We as a party remain committed to a noble art – politics. Politics has been descried as many things. Its essence is the reconciliation of differences – the greatest challenge facing the people of this community today. 'No man is good enough to govern another,' said Lincoln 'without that other man's consent.' The challenge of building a consensus in Ireland is the greatest challenge in particular to this new generation, a challenge that is all the more exciting because of the failure of previous generations to meet it. It is a challenge that will only be met by patient political negotiation. Patient political negotiation is unspectacular, it has no dramatic appeal.

'Patient political effort will not fill graves – violence will.'

The alternative – the use of violence disguised as military patriotism – has misled many young idealists. Its monuments are mangled and broken bodies, prison walls and cemeteries. Patient political effort will not fill graves – violence will. Patient political effort will not fill jails with young people. Violence will. Patient political effort will not prevent job creation in a community starved of employment, particularly for young people. Violence will. Patient political effort and non-violence have won only achievements and benefits that we can claim over the past decade. Violence has made the underlying problem – division – more difficult to solve.

Many young people have joined us in the task of politics, the difficult task of building mutual respect and understanding which forms the basis of true peace and freedom. We need many more. In the 1980s the true patriot is the builder, not the destroyer. 1981 has been a year of many lessons for many people. The SDLP has come through 1981. We hope that we shall never see its like again. Yet we have emerged with renewed strength. We can only go forward.

'I stand by the Republic.'

Des O'Malley
(b.1939)

Speech to Dáil Éireann, 20 February 1985

'I stand by the Republic.'

Moral issues loomed large over Ireland's political and social agenda in the 1980s. Society was split on questions of abortion, divorce and contraception. Political opinion was often as divided within the parties as between them.

The provision of information on family planning had been banned in the 1920s by the Cumann na nGaedheal government. The subsequent Fianna Fáil government prohibited the sale and importation of contraceptives. In 1979, the minister for health, Charles Haughey, had introduced a bill to allow the sale of contraceptives on prescription to married people. This he described as an 'Irish solution to an Irish problem'. Student union shops and family planning clinics continued to flout the law by openly selling condoms over the counter.

In 1985, Barry Desmond, minister for health in the Fine Gael/Labour coalition, introduced legislation to allow the sale of 'non-medical contraceptives' (i.e. condoms) without prescription in pharmacies, family planning clinics and surgeries. The Catholic church reacted with fury. Publicly it engaged in debate about the dangers of such a move. Privately, things were more disturbing. Many deputies spoke of a sinister campaign of threats and intimidation against them and their families.

Fianna Fáil deputies had been instructed by Charles Haughey, now party leader, to vote against Desmond's bill. While many voiced their unhappiness, only one – Limerick deputy Dessie O'Malley – stated that he would not vote with the party. Haughey had faced continual opposition from a section of Fianna Fáil since his election in 1979. O'Malley was the most vigorous and effective of his opponents.

The debate on the bill – at root a battle between liberal and conservative opinion – was predictably fraught. The most notable contribution was that of O'Malley, for whom it represented something of an apologia. He described the debate as a 'watershed in Irish politics'. It was certainly a turning point for O'Malley. Less than a

BIOGRAPHY

Des O'Malley was born in 1939 in Limerick, the nephew of Donogh O'Malley (1921–68), whom he succeeded as TD for Limerick East in 1968. As parliamentary secretary to the taoiseach, O'Malley was a staunch supporter of Jack Lynch and opponent of Charles Haughey during the Arms Crisis of 1970 during which he was appointed minister for justice. He was involved in the so-called anti-Haughey Heaves of the early 1980s before Fianna Fáil

expelled him in 1985. In 1989 he led his new party, the Progressive Democrats, into an unlikely coalition with Haughey. O'Malley finally brought down his rival in 1992, when he precipitated the resignation of Haughey as taoiseach. He retired from politics at the 2002 general election, when his cousin, Tim O'Malley, was elected in Limerick East, and his daughter, Fiona O'Malley, won Dún Laoghaire (although both lost their seats in 2007).

week later, Fianna Fáil's national executive expelled him for 'conduct unbecoming' a party member. He sat as an independent for almost a year before establishing the Progressive Democrats in January 1986. Three years later the party entered a coalition with Fianna Fáil under the leadership of taoiseach Charles Haughey.

… There are certain fundamental matters which far transcend the details of this bill and which are of grave importance to democracy on this island. I cannot ignore the principle that is involved.

Difficulties have arisen since the publication of the bill. In the past ten days or so the most extraordinary and unprecedented extra-parliamentary pressure has been brought to bear on many Members of the House. This is not merely ordinary lobbying. It is far more significant. I regret to have to say that it borders at times almost on the sinister. We have witnessed the public and the private agonies of so many Members of the House who are being asked not to make decisions on this bill in their own calm and collected judgment but to make them as a result of emotional and at times overwhelming moral pressure. This must constrain their freedom …

'This debate can be regarded as a sort of watershed.'

In many respects this debate can be regarded as a sort of watershed in Irish politics. It will have a considerable influence on the whole political institutional, democratic future, not just of these 26 counties but of the whole island. We must approach the subject very seriously and bearing that in mind. It is right to ask ourselves now what would be the reaction and the effect of this bill being defeated this evening. I am not interested in the reaction or the effect so far as contraception is concerned because that is no longer relevant. If the bill is defeated there are two elements on this island who will rejoice to high heaven. They are the unionists in Northern Ireland and the extremist Roman Catholics in the Republic. They are a curious alliance, but they are bound together by the vested interest each of them has in the perpetuation of partition. Neither wishes to know the other. Their wish is to keep this island divided. Most of us here realize that the imposition of partition on this island was a grievous wrong, but its deliberate continuation is equally a grievous wrong. No one who wishes that this island, this race and this nation be united again should try to have that division copper fastened. It does not matter what any of us might like to say to ourselves about what might be the effects of the availability of condoms or anything else, what really matters and what will matter in 10, 20 or 30 years' time is whether the elected representatives of the Irish people decided they wished to underwrite, at least mentally, the concept of partition.

Most of us in the House fervently want to see a 32-county republic on this island. I am not as optimistic as I used to be about that – I think the day is further away than it might otherwise be because of the events of the last 10 or 15 years. I am certain of one thing in relation to partition: we will never see a 32-county republic on this island until first of all we have here a 26-county republic in the part we have jurisdiction over today which is really a republic, practising real republican traditions. Otherwise, we can forget about the possibility of ever succeeding in persuading our fellow Irishmen in the North to join us ...

'Allow citizens to make their own free choice.'

In a democratic republic people should not think in terms of having laws other than those that allow citizens to make their own free choice in so far as these private matters are concerned. That is what I believe a republic should do. It should take account of the reasonable views of all groups, including all minorities, because if we do not take into account the rights of minorities here, can we complain if they are not taken into account in the other part of this island, or anywhere else ...

This whole matter affects me personally and politically. I have thought about it and agonized about it. Quite a number of deputies have been subjected to a particular type of pressure, but I am possibly unique in that I have been subjected to two enormous pressures, the more general type and a particular political one. They are both like flood tides – neither of them is easy to resist and it is probably more than twice as hard to resist the two of them. But it comes down to certain fundamentals. One has to take into account everything that has been said but one must also act in accordance with one's conscience, not on contraceptives, which is irrelevant now, but on the bigger and deeper issues that I have talked about today.

I cannot avoid acting, in my present situation, where I do not have the protection of the Whip, other than in the way I feel, giving some practical recognition at least to the kind of pressures and the entreaties of my friends for my own good, which I greatly appreciate.

I will conclude by quoting from a letter in the *Irish Times* of 16 February, signed by Father Dominic Johnson OSB, a monk of Glenstal Abbey where he says, 'With respect to Mr O'Malley, he might reflect with profit on the life of St Thomas More, who put his conscience before politics and lost his life for doing so.'

The politics of this would be very easy. The politics would be, to be one of the lads, the safest way in Ireland. But I do not believe that the interests of this state, or our constitution and of this Republic, would be served by putting politics before conscience in regard to this. There is a choice of a kind that can only be answered by saying that I stand by the Republic and accordingly I will not oppose this bill.

'*People are entitled to a mature discussion.*'

Garret FitzGerald

(b.1926)

Speech to Dáil Éireann, 16 May 1986

'People are entitled to a mature discussion.'

When it came to the issue of divorce in Ireland, it seemed for decades that W.B. Yeats would have the last word (see his speech on page 78). Once it had been rendered illegal by the Free State government in 1925, the issue was largely forgotten (although when drafting a new constitution, Éamon de Valera was careful to include a provision that 'no law shall be enacted providing for the grant of a dissolution of marriage'). Marital breakdown was a fact of Irish life – recognized in provisions such as the deserted wives allowance introduced in 1970 – but repeal of the divorce ban stayed off the agenda for successive governments of all colours. Even tentative efforts at reform – such as a 1960s committee of inquiry into the 1937 constitution (Bunreacht na hÉireann) that concluded the ban was 'a source of embarrassment' – met with such a barrage of criticism from the Catholic hierarchy that the issue was quietly parked.

In the 1980s, taoiseach and leader of Fine Gael, Garret FitzGerald, decided to take on the Catholic church by declaring his intention to repeal the ban. In the course of an interview on RTÉ radio in 1981, he announced a 'crusade' to make the state a 'genuine republic'. He promised to remove from the constitution anything that northern Protestants found unacceptable. Critics dismissed this as an exercise in gesture politics aimed at his middle-class constituents in prosperous Dublin 4. Northern Ireland Protestants seemed nonplussed, apparently caring little for the constitution or laws of their neighbouring jurisdiction. FitzGerald soon caved in to pressure by Catholic lobby groups on most issues, not least in agreeing to a referendum on a new amendment to the constitution protecting the 'unborn'.

In 1985, after a damning report by an all-party committee on marriage breakdown, the government finally decided to grasp the nettle on divorce. The debate about whether a referendum, opposed by Fianna Fáil, should even take place was one of the bitterest ever held in the Dáil. FitzGerald's speech on 16 May 1986 focused on the importance of allowing those who had experienced marital breakdown to regularize their situation. References to opinion in Northern Ireland provided echoes of his constitutional crusade. Ultimately, the

BIOGRAPHY

Garret FitzGerald was born in Dublin in 1926, the son of Desmond FitzGerald, the first minister for external affairs of the Irish Free State. Educated at Belvedere College and University College Dublin, he lectured in economics at UCD from 1959. Elected to the Seanad in 1965, he became a TD four years later. Despite his difficult relationship with the Fine Gael leader and taoiseach, Liam Cosgrave, he was appointed minister for foreign affairs in 1973. Succeeding Cosgrave as party leader in 1977, FitzGerald briefly formed a minority coalition government in 1981, and a majority one in 1982–7. He resigned as party leader after defeat at the 1987 general election, and retired from the Dáil in 1992. His memoir *All in a Life* was a bestseller.

amendment to remove the ban failed, but it was an important part of a broader movement towards a more pluralistic Ireland.

It was almost ten years before a second attempt was made to remove the prohibition on divorce. The referendum was passed by a margin of less than one per cent.

… As legislators elected by the people, we have, I believe, a duty of leadership in relation to this matter as we have in other matters; and we in the parties in government are exercising this leadership by proposing a very restrictive form of divorce with a minimal impact on existing marriages, which will at the same time reduce the destabilizing effect of marriage breakdown on society, so as to increase the stability of family life in our society.

On the merits of this proposition there are not merely deeply divided opinions; there are deeply divided approaches to the whole matter, involving the application of quite different criteria to the issue involved. The first of these approaches involves the application of the criterion of the social good. I believe that this is in fact the most important criteria that we should apply to this issue, because of the social nature of marriage itself …

A second approach emphasizes the importance of respect for diversity of opinion and for freedom under the law. These are very important values which must command the respect of the state, in conjunction with the issue of the social good.

'The social nature of marriage itself.'

A third approach, distinguishable I believe from the second, emphasizes the importance of compassion in human affairs. Despite the old adage that bad cases make bad law, we cannot ignore this human value, which must be given its place within the overall social good.

A fourth approach, which has the support of a minority here even though it has been repeatedly repudiated by the authorities of the Roman Catholic Church, is that the theology and law of that church should be the foundation of, or even constitute the content of, the civil law of our state. While personally committed to the indissoluble character of sacramental marriage in the church of which I am a member, I reject that approach, in common with the authorities of my church and the vast majority of the Irish people.

In this debate we should try to disentangle these different approaches and to consider what weight should be given to each of them. Otherwise the debate could be a dialogue of the deaf, involving nothing more than repetitive reassertions of extreme positions. On the one side there could be a series of reiterations of the 'conservative' position, namely, that divorce is contrary to the theology, and at variance with the ecclesiastical law of the Roman Catholic Church, and that it would destabilize society – without any consideration of the alternative social danger that our society might be even more destabilized by a continuation of the present situation. On the other side there could be an equally tedious reiteration of the 'liberal' position that there is an individual 'right' to divorce – without regard either to the losses as well as gains involved for individuals, or to the possible social consequences of a change in the *status quo*.

I recognize that no single contribution to the discussion, nor even a sustained effort to secure rational debate, will necessarily succeed in an area that arouses such strong emotions on either side. But it is our duty in this House as elected leaders of opinion, responsible both for the common good and for the protection of individual rights, to attempt to place the debate on a rational level, and to follow, indeed, the good advice of the Roman Catholic hierarchy that 'in this debate opposing views should be fairly stated and honestly listened to and appraised' …

'The importance of compassion in human affairs.'

I believe that, given that the balance of stability in society will be enhanced rather than reduced, we can properly have regard also to the enhancement of respect for diversity of opinion and for freedom which this measure will also bring with it, as well as to the fact that this measure has a compassionate aspect that is appropriate to a caring society … Our people are entitled to such a mature discussion in their Parliament. They are entitled to the considered advice of their legislators as to the impact of this constitutional amendment on marriage and on our society. Our party have determined that they will have the benefit of this advice, and that in the public discussion that will follow the passing of this amendment by the Houses of the Oireachtas, we shall give the necessary leadership to ensure that the electorate can themselves deliver a balanced verdict on the proposal being submitted for their decision.

'This debate has also an importance that extends outside the boundaries of this state.'

In conclusion, I believe that this debate has also an importance that extends outside the boundaries of this state. The type of provision we are proposing to make for divorce takes account of lessons to be learned from other countries, and may, I believe, come to be seen elsewhere as a balanced and mature approach to a difficult problem. This debate, and the subsequent wider public discussion, together with the eventual decision taken by the people of this state, will, of course, be watched particularly closely by people of both traditions in Northern Ireland, many of whom will, I believe, be influenced to a degree in their attitude towards this state and towards each other by the manner in which we act in this matter.

'They will also be helping incidentally the relationship between North and South.'

That will not be a primary consideration when this matter is put to the test. But it should not be ignored either. And to the extent that electors conclude that this proposal should be adopted on its own merits to meet the social needs of this state, to that extent they will also be helping incidentally the relationship between North and South and between the communities in Northern Ireland. At a time when the situation in Northern Ireland is so delicately balanced this is not something we can reasonably ignore.

'*I will not play that game.*'

Alan Dukes

(b.1945)

Speech at Tallaght, South Dublin, 2 September 1987

Charles Haughey understood in 1980 that Ireland had been living 'beyond its means', but he had shied away from the brutal cuts needed to stop the spiral of decline. Public spending remained out of control. The national debt hit 1.5 times GNP. Unemployment and emigration continued to rocket. Little changed when a Fine Gael/Labour coalition under Garret FitzGerald came to power in December 1982. Elements within Fine Gael favoured spending cuts, but Labour vehemently opposed them. By 1987, after five bitter years in government, the two parties were at each other's throats. Fine Gael went into the general election on a courageous manifesto of savage cuts in public spending, borrowing and wage rates for young people. The party's vote fell by 12 per cent.

Fianna Fáil were returned as the largest party, but, short of a majority, it could only form a minority administration. It had spent much of the previous five years opposing even modest cutbacks. In office it proposed reductions that were brutal. Deadlock seemed inevitable, but on 2 September 1987 the new Fine Gael leader, Alan Dukes, stunned everyone with a speech at Tallaght that promised support for the government so long as it adopted a responsible economic policy in the national interest.

This kind of bipartisan approach between Fine Gael and Fianna Fáil was highly unusual in Irish politics. Dukes was scarcely given any credit for it at the time. The policy lasted until 1990, when Fine Gael fired their leader and abandoned his 'Tallaght strategy'. Many years afterwards Charles Haughey acknowledged that Dukes's contribution had been 'enormously important' in giving him an opportunity to get the economy back on track. Dukes was not father to the emerging 'Celtic tiger', but could justifiably claim that he opened the door at the maternity hospital for the expectant mother.

BIOGRAPHY

Alan Dukes was born in Dublin in 1945 and educated by the Christian Brothers and at University College Dublin. An economist with the Irish Farmers Association in Brussels, he eventually became chief of staff to Ireland's European commissioner, Dick Burke. Elected to Dáil Éireann in 1981, Dukes became minister for agriculture on his first day in Leinster House. He succeeded Garret FitzGerald as Fine Gael leader in 1987, but was ousted by John Bruton in 1990 after poor election results. He lost his seat in 2002 and subsequently became director-general of the Dublin think-tank, the Institute of European Affairs.

The essential task facing us in Ireland today is to find successful and sustainable ways of:

Expanding employment

Stimulating economic growth

Eliminating deprivation in our society

Removing inequities from our economic and social system

I am concerned, above all, with the lives and livelihoods of Irish people. I am concerned with finding ways to improve people's lives and to increase their chances of making a livelihood in the economic and social circumstances that surround them …

It is the role of the government to create the conditions in which all of these issues can be successfully addressed.

'I am concerned, above all, with the lives and livelihoods of Irish people.'

It is the role of the parliamentary Opposition to ensure that the government does this, to redirect government policy where it diverges from the right track, and to oppose government policy where it is wrong. That is the core of my role as leader of the Opposition. In specific terms, that means that, when the government is moving in the right, overall direction, I will not oppose the central thrust of its policy. If it is going in the right direction, I do not believe that it should be deviated from its course, or tripped up on macro-economical issues. Specifically, it means that, if in 1988 the government introduces a budget which:

Opens the way to a reduction in taxes and particularly to a reduction in personal taxes

Brings about a significant reduction in the current budget deficit below the figure targeted for this year

Holds out a strategy for real employment expansion in future years

Does not add to the burden of debt service costs in future years

I will not oppose the general thrust of its policy. No other policy of opposition will conform to the real needs of Irish people: any other policy of opposition would amount simply to a cynical exploitation of short-term political opportunities for a political advantage which would inevitably prove to be equally shortlived. I will not play that game, because it would not produce any real or lasting advantage for the Irish people – least of all for those who currently have neither political nor economic advantage.

'An obligation on government to listen.'

The reality of Irish life today requires the Opposition to accept responsibility: it also places an obligation on government to listen …

I have been struck by the extraordinarily destructive effect of old-style opposition over the last five years. An Opposition which knows very well the depth of our problems but which encourages every interest group to oppose the government is betraying its political role. An Opposition which acts in a way that makes every step forward more painful than it needs to be is perverting its function. An Opposition which tries, in our times, to say that corrective action is unnecessary is betraying the Irish people.

'I have no doubt that we can surmount our economic difficulties.'

I will not play the political game which produces the sort of phoney economic analysis which has passed for opposition in the past. I am in opposition – I would rather be in government. But I will not pretend that economic reality has changed just because I now find myself in opposition.

I have no doubt that we can surmount our economic difficulties. We will do it by adopting the realistic approach which I have set out. We will do it by consciously deciding to work together.

To sum up: it is clear that any real, concerned and compassionate response to the issues facing us requires that our public finance problem be vigorously addressed; I will support the general thrust of budgetary and economic policies designed with this in mind; within that framework, we must give priority to cases and situations of deprivation and real need; this will involve the Opposition, as well as the government, in making enlightened choices and decisions. That is the way my party will conduct its business: I challenge the other parties who have accepted the view of the economy which I have proposed and defended for six years to follow my approach.

'Come dance with me in Ireland.'

Mary Robinson
(b.1944)

Speech at Dublin Castle, 3 December 1990

For much of the history of the Irish state, the presidency was something of an old boys' club for superannuated politicians. This notion seemed particularly apposite throughout the 1980s during the self-effacing presidency of Dr Patrick Hillery. As Hillery's second and final term neared its end in 1990, the Labour Party decided to shake up the system. Even putting up a candidate was significant, since Labour had never before contested the presidential election. This guaranteed that there would have to be a contest. (Hillery had been unopposed in 1976 and 1983). Yet it was Labour's choice of a female candidate that was truly out of the ordinary.

Mary Robinson, a senior counsel and former Reid professor of law in Trinity College, had associated herself with the movement for the liberalization of Irish law and society. She had as a young senator in 1970 sponsored legislation to legalize contraception, and had latterly been active in the campaign to decriminalize homosexuality.

The presidential contest was controversial and thrilling. Brian Lenihan, the genial Fianna Fáil tánaiste (deputy prime minister), was odds-on favourite for most of the campaign. Robinson seemed likely to achieve a respectable second place, with Fine Gael's Austin Currie trailing a distant third. But Lenihan's campaign imploded when a postgraduate student released an interview with the candidate he had recorded while researching his Master's thesis at University College Dublin. Lenihan revealed, despite previous denials, that he had attempted to make contact with President Hillery to ask him not to dissolve the Dáil when the FitzGerald government had been defeated on its budget in January 1982. Nine days before the presidential election, facing an opposition motion of no confidence and with the Progressive Democrats threatening to withdraw from the coalition, Haughey dismissed Lenihan as tánaiste. Matters were made worse for Lenihan by a personal attack on Robinson by Fianna Fáil's Padraig Flynn that caused widespread offence.

Lenihan, who remained a popular figure with the Fianna Fáil grass roots, still won the highest number of first preferences on polling day. Robinson was elected on Currie's transfers. It was a watershed moment: for a woman viewed as the personification of the 'liberal agenda' to be elected head of state seemed to proclaim a social revolution.

Eoghan Harris, the *Sunday Independent* commentator who had put his mastery

BIOGRAPHY

Mary Robinson was born in Ballina, County Mayo, in 1944. She was educated at Trinity College, Dublin, where she subsequently became, aged 25, the youngest Reid professor of constitutional law. After 20 years in Seanad Éireann, she was inaugurated as the seventh (and first female) president of Ireland on 3 December 1990. Robinson was the first head of state to visit Somalia following the crisis there in 1992, and to visit Rwanda in the aftermath of the 1994 genocide. She resigned on 12 September 1997 to become United Nations High Commissioner for Human Rights, a post she held until 2002.

of political rhetoric at Robinson's disposal, kept his best soundbite for the victory rally. 'The women of Ireland, *mná na hÉireann*,' the president-elect declared, 'instead of rocking the cradle rocked the system.' Fergus Finlay of her campaign team later recalled these as 'words crafted by a genius'.

The 'system rocked' was a theme to which Robinson returned in this inaugural address. 'The Ireland I will be representing,' she promised, 'is a new Ireland: open, tolerant, inclusive.'

Citizens of Ireland, *mná na hÉireann agus fir na hÉireann* [the women of Ireland and the men of Ireland], you have chosen me to represent you and I am humbled by and grateful for your trust. The Ireland I will be representing is a new Ireland, open, tolerant, inclusive. Many of you who voted for me did so without sharing all my views. This, I believe, is a significant signal of change, a sign, however modest, that we have already passed the threshold to a new, pluralist Ireland.

The recent revival of an old concept of the Fifth Province expresses this emerging Ireland of tolerance and empathy. The old Irish term for province is *coicead*, meaning 'fifth'; and yet, as everyone knows, there are only four geographical provinces on this island. So where is the fifth? The Fifth Province is not anywhere here or there, north or south, east or west. It is a place within each of us – that place that is open to the other, that swinging door which allows us to venture out and others to venture in. Ancient legends divide Ireland into four quarters and a 'middle', although they differed about the location of this middle or Fifth Province. While Tara was the political centre of Ireland, tradition has it that this Fifth Province acted as a second centre, a necessary balance. If I am a symbol of anything I would like to be a symbol of this reconciling and healing Fifth Province.

'The West's awake.'

My primary role as president will be to represent this state. But the state is not the only model of community with which Irish people can and do identify. Beyond our state there is a vast community of Irish emigrants extending not only across our neighbouring island – which has provided a home away from home for several Irish generations – but also throughout the continents of North America, Australia and of course Europe itself. There are over 70 million people living on this globe who claim Irish descent. I will be proud to represent them. And I would like to see Áras an Uachtaráin, my official residence, serve – on something of an annual basis – as a place where our emigrant communities could send representatives for a get-together of the extended Irish family abroad …

If it is time, as Joyce's Stephen Dedalus remarked, that the Irish began to forge in the smithy of our souls 'the uncreated conscience of our race' – might we not take on the still 'uncreated conscience' of the wider international community? Is it not time that the small started believing again that it is beautiful, that the periphery can rise up and speak out on equal terms with the centre, that the most outlying island community of the European Community really has something 'strange and precious' to contribute to the sea-change presently sweeping through the entire continent of Europe? As a native of Ballina, one of the most western towns of the most western province of the most western nation in Europe, I want to say – 'the West's awake'.

I turn now to another place close to my heart, Northern Ireland. As the elected choice of the people of this part of our island I want to extend the hand of friendship and of love to both communities in the other part. And I want to do this with no hidden agendas, no strings attached. As the person chosen by you to symbolize this Republic and to project our self-image to others, I will seek to encourage mutual understanding and tolerance between all the different communities sharing this island.

'I want women who have felt themselves outside history to be written back into history.'

In seeking to do this I shall rely to a large extent on symbols. But symbols are what unite and divide people. Symbols give us our identity, our self-image, our way of explaining ourselves to ourselves and to others. Symbols in turn determine the kinds of stories we tell; and the stories we tell determine the kind of history we make and remake. I want Áras an Uachtaráin to be a place where people can tell diverse stories – in the knowledge that there is someone there to listen.

I want this presidency to promote the telling of stories – stories of celebration through the arts and stories of conscience and of social justice. As a woman, I want women who have felt themselves outside history to be written back into history, in the words of Eavan Boland, 'finding a voice where they found a vision'.

May God direct me so that my presidency is one of justice, peace and love. May I have the fortune to preside over an Ireland at a time of exciting transformation when we enter a new Europe where old wounds can be healed, a time when, in the words of Seamus Heaney, 'hope and history rhyme'. May it be a presidency where I, the president, can sing to you, citizens of Ireland, the joyous refrain of the 14th-century Irish poet as recalled by W.B. Yeats, 'I am of Ireland … come dance with me in Ireland.'

'*A necessary development of human rights.*'

Máire Geoghegan-Quinn

(b.1950)

Speech to Dáil Éireann, 23 June 1993

The culture wars that gripped Ireland in the 1980s and early 1990s included a number of set-piece battles between the forces of liberalism and conservatism. Gay rights was one such confrontation.

Sex between men was illegal under Victorian laws that had been carried over into independent Ireland. In the early 1980s, David Norris, an academic at Trinity College and a prominent gay rights activist, argued in the Supreme Court that the legislation was unconstitutional. He made a case that the laws interfered with his right to privacy and cited a decision by the European Court of Human Rights that upheld an appeal against the criminalization of homosexual acts in Northern Ireland. In April 1983, a majority decision of the Supreme Court found against Norris on the basis that the constitution guaranteed privacy only within marriage. It also found that the domestic Supreme Court was superior to the European court.

Norris appealed the judgment to the European Court of Human Rights, which found in his favour in 1988. Obliged by international law to repeal the offending legislation, successive governments simply ignored the ruling. In 1993, Máire Geoghegan-Quinn, minister for justice in a Fianna Fáil/Labour coalition, controversially moved to introduce a bill to decriminalize sexual acts between consenting male adults.

The bill came before the Dáil in the wake of a barrage of moral controversies. 'We are in an era in which values are being examined and questioned,' Geoghegan-Quinn noted on 23 June, 'and that it is no more than our duty as legislators to show that we appreciate what is happening.' The bill decriminalized homosexual acts and, by establishing a common age of consent, effectively made homosexual and heterosexual acts equal in the eyes of the law. This was not 'an Irish solution to an Irish problem'. Rather, said the minister, it was 'a necessary development of human rights'.

Though opposed by many Catholic groups and some in Fianna Fáil, the bill passed without a division. The forthright manner in which Geoghegan-Quinn introduced the legislation earned her the plaudits of the gay community and liberal opinion beyond.

> **BIOGRAPHY**
>
> **Máire Geoghegan-Quinn** was born in 1950 in Carna, County Galway, the daughter of the Fianna Fáil deputy for Galway West, Johnny Geoghegan, whom she succeeded in 1975. In 1979 she became the first woman cabinet minister since the foundation of the state. In 1991, she resigned from the government in opposition to Charles Haughey's leadership. She returned in 1992 under Albert Reynolds, and as minister for justice in 1993 helped to negotiate the Joint Declaration on Peace and Reconciliation in Ireland with the British government. She retired from politics in 1997, following which she was appointed to the European Court of Auditors.

'A necessary development of human rights.'

The primary purpose of this bill, which forms part of a comprehensive programme of reform of the criminal law which I have under way at present, is to decriminalize sexual activity between consenting mature males. The bill also contains a series of measures designed to protect the vulnerable; and to review and update the law on prostitution and related offences with particular emphasis on sanctions in relation to the clients of prostitutes and those who organize prostitution. While it is the case that the main sections of the bill arise against a background of the European Court decision in the Norris case, it would be a pity to use that judgment as the sole pretext for the action we are now taking so as to avoid facing up to the issues themselves.

'We are seeking to end … discrimination.'

What we are concerned with fundamentally in this bill is a necessary development of human rights. We are seeking to end that form of discrimination which says that those whose nature is to express themselves sexually in their personal relationships, as consenting adults, in a way which others disapprove of or feel uneasy about, must suffer the sanctions of the criminal law. We are saying in 1993, over 130 years since that section of criminal law was enacted, that it is time we brought this form of human rights limitation to an end. We are recognizing that we are in an era in which values are being examined and questioned and that it is no more than our duty as legislators to show that we appreciate what is happening by dismantling a law which reflects the values of another time.

'As a people we have proved our ability to adopt a balanced and mature approach in dealing with complex social issues.'

That process of change is not easy and, understandably, many people worry that the traditional values which they hold so dear, and many of which are fundamentally sound, are under siege from emerging modern realities. But, of course, it is not a matter of laying siege to all the old certainties, nor is it a matter of jettisoning sound values simply to run with a current tide of demand, which may or may not be a majority demand. It is, rather, a matter of closely looking at values and asking ourselves whether it is necessary, or right, that they be propped up for the comfort of the majority by applying discriminatory and unnecessary laws to a minority, any minority.

As a people we have proved our ability to adopt a balanced and mature approach in dealing with complex social issues. In this context I am particularly pleased to note that, by and large, the public debate which has taken place in relation to the area covered by the bill has been marked by a lack of stridency and by a respect for the sincerity of the views held by others.

Because some of the issues raised by this bill are ones on which many people have deeply and sincerely held opposing views, it is perhaps inevitable that in the public debate the reality of what the bill actually proposes to do can sometimes be lost sight of in the context of wider issues which tend to be raised. For this reason it is important to emphasize that the House is not being asked to take a view as to whether sexual behaviour of the kind dealt with in the main sections of the bill should be regarded as morally or socially acceptable. Instead, what is simply at issue is whether it is right in this day and age that the full force and sanctions of the criminal law should be available in relation to such forms of sexual behaviour.

'We have come to appreciate the need to recognize, respect and value difference.'

Majority values do not require that kind of support and I believe this is something that each of us knows instinctively. We know in ourselves also that values which are truly worthwhile in themselves are strengthened – not weakened – when we remove forms of apparent support which ignore the rights of others. In other areas of public concern and debate in this country we have come to appreciate the need to recognize, respect and value difference. This House needs no reminding of the tragedy which ensues when difference is deprived the right of expression and suppressed …

I do not believe that it is any answer to say that in practice these laws are rarely if ever implemented and we would be best to leave well enough alone. Such an approach would be dishonest, could bring the law generally into disrepute and, it seems to me, would be grossly and gratuitously offensive to those who happen to be homosexual. Genuine tolerance is not achieved by the turning of a blind eye. The social acceptability of homosexuality is not something which by our laws we can decree; the hurt which homosexuals feel at their treatment as outcasts by some members of the community is not something which we can dispel by the use of some legislative magic wand. What we can do under the terms of this bill is leave those of homosexual orientation free to come to terms with their lives and express themselves in personal relationships without the fear of being branded and being punished as criminals …

Most of the legislation which it is proposed to repeal in this bill is, by any standards, ancient. One glance at the schedule of repeals will reveal references to acts of 1842, 1847, 1861 and so on. Of course, just because legislation is old is not in itself a valid reason for repealing it. However, where it is outdated, or inoperable or simply unacceptable because of the language used, being language of another age, we have a valid reason for repealing.

'Rolling back over 130 years of legislative prohibition which is discriminatory.'

While inevitably much of the public attention which has been given to this bill has concentrated on the issue of homosexuality, the other provisions which I have outlined – particularly in relation to the protection of the vulnerable and the emphasis on sanctions against clients of prostitutes and those who organize prostitution – will also be seen as worthwhile and substantial changes to our law. Overall the bill is a balanced, measured and enlightened approach to the sensitive and difficult issues with which it deals. It is right that we should take the opportunity, now, of rolling back over 130 years of legislative prohibition which is discriminatory, which reflects an inadequate understanding of the human condition and which we should, rightly, see as an impediment, not a prop, to the maintenance and development of sound social values and norms.

'The Ireland I now inhabit.'

Séamus Heaney
(b.1939)

Speech in Stockholm, 7 December 1995

The Irish have often punched above their weight in international competitions, not least the Eurovision song contest, Miss World and Nobel prizes. The latter included five for peace, two for physics and four for literature. Of the writers, the work of Beckett and Shaw was not rooted in Ireland, nor particularly shaped by it. In contrast, the work of Yeats and Heaney was suffused with Irish history and culture. Both men lived in Ireland at times of upheaval: Yeats through the troubles of the early part of the century, Heaney those which came later.

Heaney had been tipped as a Nobel laureate for years. The committee's decision to award him the 1995 prize was striking in that it coincided with the early years of the Northern Ireland peace process. Heaney's poetry in the 1970s had engaged with Catholic identity and the 'troubles', most famously in his 1975 collection *North*. Although since the 1980s he had moved on to other themes and classically based translations, it was his work on Northern Ireland that the Nobel committee commended when bestowing the prize. 'As an Irish Catholic,' his citation noted, 'he has concerned himself with analysis of the violence in Northern Ireland – with the express reservation that he wants to avoid the conventional terms.'

Heaney was on holiday in Greece when the news broke and it was some time before he could be found. Doubtless he was a little more gracious on receiving word than his predecessor, Yeats, who had immediately inquired how much it was worth.

In his acceptance speech Heaney emphasized the influence of poetry on the individual and society. Echoing the words of Yeats, who had spoken of how 'the local work of poets and dramatists had been as important to the transformation of his native place and times as the ambushes of guerrilla armies,' Heaney paid tribute to his own contemporaries who had helped 'imagine' modern Irish society.

BIOGRAPHY

Séamus Heaney was born in April 1939, the first of nine children. His father owned and worked a small farm of 50 acres in County Derry in Northern Ireland. Heaney won a scholarship to St Columb's College, the Catholic boarding school in Derry, and went on to Queen's University, Belfast. He has held prestigious teaching appointments on both sides of the Atlantic, including at Harvard, Berkeley and Oxford. His many acclaimed publications include the prize-winning *District and Circle*, *North* and a translation of *Beowulf*. Heaney was awarded the Nobel Prize for literature in 1995.

6 … When the poet W.B. Yeats stood on this platform more than 70 years ago, Ireland was emerging from the throes of a traumatic civil war that had followed fast on the heels of a war of independence fought against the British. The struggle that ensued had been brief enough; it was over by May, 1923, some seven months before Yeats sailed to Stockholm, but it was bloody, savage and intimate, and for generations to come it would dictate the terms of

politics within the 26 independent counties of Ireland, that part of the island known first of all as the Irish Free State and then subsequently as the Republic of Ireland.

Yeats barely alluded to the civil war or the war of independence in his Nobel speech. Nobody understood better than he the connection between the construction or destruction of state institutions and the founding or foundering of cultural life, but on this occasion he chose to talk instead about the Irish Dramatic Movement. His story was about the creative purpose of that movement and its historic good fortune in having not only his own genius to sponsor it, but also the genius of his friends John Millington Synge and Lady Augusta Gregory. He came to Sweden to tell the world that the local work of poets and dramatists had been as important to the transformation of his native place and times as the ambushes of guerrilla armies; and his boast in that elevated prose was essentially the same as the one he would make in verse more than a decade later in his poem 'The municipal gallery revisited'. There Yeats presents himself amongst the portraits and heroic narrative paintings which celebrate the events and personalities of recent history and all of a sudden realizes that something truly epoch-making has occurred: '"This is not", I say, / "The dead Ireland of my youth, but an Ireland / The poets have imagined, terrible and gay."' And the poem concludes with two of the most quoted lines of his entire oeuvre:

> Think where man's glory most begins and ends,
> And say my glory was I had such friends.

And yet, expansive and thrilling as these lines are, they are an instance of poetry flourishing itself rather than proving itself, they are the poet's lap of honour, and in this respect if in no other they resemble what I am doing in this lecture. In fact, I should quote here on my own behalf some other words from the poem: 'You that would judge me, do not judge alone / This book or that.' Instead, I ask you to do what Yeats asked his audience to do and think of the achievement of Irish poets and dramatists and novelists over the past 40 years, among whom I am proud to count great friends.

'The Ireland I now inhabit is one that these Irish contemporaries have helped to imagine.'

In literary matters, Ezra Pound advised against accepting the opinion of those 'who haven't themselves produced notable work', and it is advice I have been privileged to follow, since it is the good opinion of notable workers and not just those in my own country that has fortified my endeavour since I began to write in Belfast more than 30 years ago. The Ireland I now inhabit is one that these Irish contemporaries have helped to imagine…

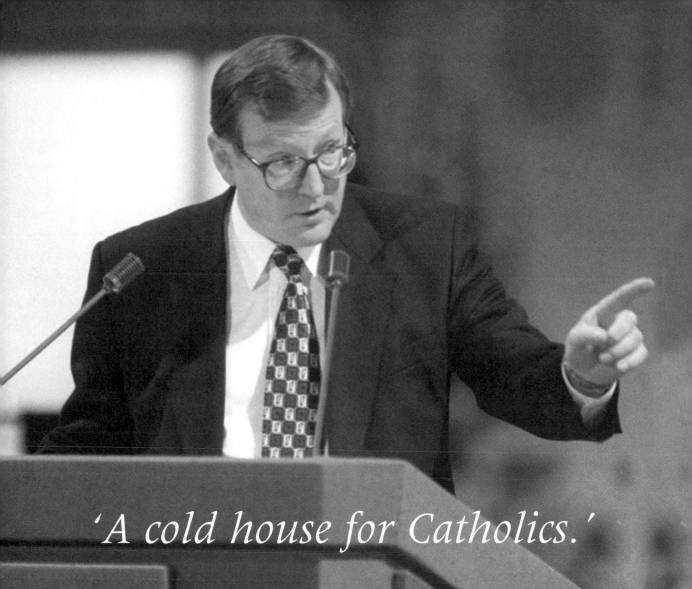

'*A cold house for Catholics.*'

David Trimble
(b.1944)

Speech in Oslo, 10 December 1998

On Good Friday, 10 April 1998, the leaders of most of Northern Ireland's political parties (excepting the Democratic Unionist Party), and the British and Irish governments signed the Belfast Agreement. It provided for a devolved, power-sharing government in Northern Ireland and included significant compromises on all sides. For republicans, it meant accepting something much less than a united Ireland (Séamus Mallon of the SDLP described it as 'Sunningdale for slow learners'). In turn, unionists consented to share government with parties aligned to paramilitaries and to the early release of political prisoners. The agreement was ratified soon afterwards by large majorities on both sides of the border, by two out of three voters in Northern Ireland and almost 100 per cent in the Republic.

Relief among supporters of the agreement was shortlived. No sooner had the referenda passed than the process came up against the stumbling block of paramilitary decommissioning. The timing could hardly have been worse. For the fourth year running, the Orange Order (which had opposed the agreement) set up camp around Drumcree church in south Armagh. Restrictions had been imposed on their traditional marching route through the Garvaghy Road in Portadown. The stand-off only ended when, on 12 July, loyalists burned down a local Catholic family's home, killing three young boys as they slept.

Republican rejectionists were also active, with a breakaway group calling itself the Real IRA planting a series of car bombs that summer. On Saturday 15 August they set off a device on the main street in Omagh without issuing a warning. The explosion caused carnage. Twenty-nine people died, including a woman pregnant with twins. It was the worst single atrocity in the history of the 'troubles'.

Violence did not encourage a spirit of reconciliation. The political process remained stalled on decommissioning. Unionists demanded that the IRA give up its arms; the IRA refused to do so. The deadline of 31 October for the formation of the Northern Ireland Executive came and went without progress.

The decision in this context by the Nobel committee to award David Trimble (and SDLP leader, John Hume) the Nobel Peace Prize proved highly controversial. Many felt it was premature. Others

BIOGRAPHY

David Trimble was born in Bangor, County Down, in 1944. He was a prominent critic of the unionist leadership during the 1970s, and only joined the Ulster Unionist Party in 1979. He was elected to Westminster in 1990 and became party leader in 1995. Despite having been a critic of the earlier Hume–Adams talks, he participated in the multi-party negotiations that resulted in the Good Friday Agreement in 1998 (the year he won the Nobel Peace Prize). Between 1999 and 2002, he twice held the position of first minister. He resigned as party leader after disastrous results at the 2005 general elections, which saw the Ulster Unionists eclipsed as the majority voice of unionism by Ian Paisley's DUP.

thought Trimble's nomination problematic at a time when he seemed a major roadblock to peace, and they questioned whether he had, as the Nobel committee's citation claimed, 'showed great political courage'. Trimble's speech – an ode to constitutionalism and democracy – was a robust response to these critics. More significant, perhaps, was something approaching an apology on behalf of unionism. Northern Ireland, he conceded, had in the past been 'a cold house for Catholics'.

... This is what I have tried to do: to tell unionists to give things a chance to develop. Given that the Ulster British people are coming out of the experience of 25 years of 'armed struggle' directed against them, they have given our appeals a generous hearing. Critics say that concessions are a sign of weakness. Burke, however says, 'Magnanimity in politics is not seldom the truest wisdom; and a great empire and little minds go ill together.' Prophetic words when we think of the history of the British Empire ...

'The decommissioning of hearts.'

But common sense dictates that I cannot for ever convince society that real peace is at hand if there is not a beginning to the decommissioning of weapons as an earnest of the decommissioning of hearts that must follow. Any further delay will reinforce dark doubts about whether Sinn Féin are drinking from the clear stream of democracy, or is still drinking from the dark stream of fascism. It cannot for ever face both ways. Plenty of space has been given to the paramilitaries. Now, winter is here, and there is still no sign of spring.

Like John Bunyan's Pilgrim, we politicians have been through the Slough of Despond. We have seen Doubting Castle, the owner whereof was Giant Despair. I can certainly recall passing many times through the Valley of Humiliation. And all too often we have encountered, not only on the other side, but on our own side too, 'the man who could look no way but downwards, with a muckrake in his hand'. Nevertheless, like one of Beckett's characters, 'I will go on, because I must go on.'

What we democratic politicians want in Northern Ireland is not some utopian society but a normal society. The best way to secure that normalcy is the tried and trusted method of parliamentary democracy. So the Northern Ireland Assembly is the primary institutional instrument for the development of a normal society in Northern Ireland. Like any Parliament it needs to be more than a cockpit for competing victimizations. Burke said it best, 'Parliament is not a congress of ambassadors from different and hostile interests; which interests each must maintain, as an agent and an advocate, against other agents and advocates; but Parliament is a deliberative assembly of one nation, with one interest, that of the whole; where not local purposes, nor local prejudices ought to guide, but the general good resulting from the general reason of the whole.'

Some critics complain that I lack 'the vision thing'. But vision in its pure meaning is clear sight. That does not mean I have no dreams. I do. But I try to have them at night. By day I am satisfied if I can see the furthest limit of what is possible. Politics can be likened to driving at night over unfamiliar hills and mountains … There are hills in Northern Ireland and there are mountains. The hills are decommissioning and policing. But the mountain, if we could but see it clearly, is not in front of us but behind us, in history. The dark shadow we seem to see in the distance is not really a mountain ahead, but the shadow of the mountain behind – a shadow from the past thrown forward into our future. It is a dark sludge of historical sectarianism. We can leave it behind us if we wish.

'Politics can be likened to driving at night over unfamiliar hills and mountains.'

But both communities must leave it behind, because both created it. Each thought it had good reason to fear the other. As Namier says, the irrational is not necessarily unreasonable. Ulster Unionists, fearful of being isolated on the island, built a solid house, but it was a cold house for Catholics. And northern nationalists, although they had a roof over their heads, seemed to us as if they meant to burn the house down. None of us are entirely innocent. But thanks to our strong sense of civil society, thanks to our religious recognition that none of us are perfect, thanks to the thousands of people from both sides who made countless acts of good authority, thanks to a tradition of parliamentary democracy which meant that paramilitarism never displaced politics, thanks to all these specific, concrete circumstances we, thank god, stopped short of that abyss that engulfed Bosnia, Kosovo, Somalia and Rwanda … There are two traditions in Northern Ireland. There are two main religious denominations. But there is only one true moral denomination. And it wants peace.

'*Closer to Boston than Berlin.*'

Mary Harney
(b.1953)

*Speech at a meeting of the American Bar Association in the
Law Society of Ireland, Blackhall Place, Dublin, 21 July 2000*

The Irish electorate voted by a large majority in May 1972 to join the European Economic Community. Membership had been a key goal of Fianna Fáil governments under Seán Lemass and Jack Lynch. Of the mainstream parties only Labour had demurred. Most politicians correctly judged that Europe would be good for Ireland. The common agricultural policy and infrastructural funds would eventually boost the country's economy. European law, particularly equality legislation, encouraged a process of liberalization and pluralism. Further referenda – in 1987 on the Single European Act and in 1992 on the Maastricht Treaty – demonstrated that opposition to 'ever closer union' existed only at the margins of political life. With Ireland a beneficiary of the EU largesse, there seemed little reason to jump off the gravy train.

BIOGRAPHY

Mary Harney was born in Ballinasloe, County Galway, in 1953 and educated at Trinity College, Dublin. In entering political life in 1977 as a senate nominee of taoiseach Jack Lynch, Harney became the youngest-ever member of Seanad Éireann. Elected to the Dáil in 1981, she left Fianna Fáil in 1985 to co-found the Progressive Democrats (PDs). Harney took over the leadership of the party in 1993 and entered a Fianna Fáil–PD coalition government four years later, becoming Ireland's first female tánaiste. In 2006, she resigned the party leadership, but, after a catastrophic showing by the PDs at the election the following year (which saw new leader, Michael McDowell, lose his seat), Harney returned to lead the party into coalition government with Fianna Fáil and the Green Party.

Only in the late 1990s did cracks appear in this mainstream consensus. Foremost among the Eurosceptics was Fianna Fáil finance minister, Charlie McCreevey, who was highly critical of the fiscal restraints imposed upon him by the European Central Bank. His Progressive Democrats coalition partner, enterprise minister Mary Harney, supported him. Both regarded low corporate tax rates and the resulting foreign direct investment from the United States as the crucial factor in the renowned 'Celtic tiger'. 'Our economic success,' said Harney in this speech to the American Bar Association on 21 July 2000, 'owes more to American liberalism than to European leftism.'

Harney's statement that Ireland was 'a lot closer to Boston than Berlin' resonated in a country tiring of the European experiment. Her words immediately entered the Irish political lexicon as shorthand for the battle of ideas between economic liberalism and corporatism. Few doubted where the tánaiste herself stood in that conflict. She demanded a 'proper debate in Ireland about the issue of further European integration', accusing the traditional EU states, particularly Germany and France, of being 'wedded to an outmoded philosophy of high taxation and heavy regulation which condemns millions of their people to unemployment'. She did not 'want to see a situation in Ireland where we have to import the kind of job-destroying policies which are keeping millions of people on the dole right across continental Europe'.

Harney's speech marked a turning point in Ireland's waning love affair with the European Union.

History and geography have placed Ireland in a very special position between America and Europe.

History has bound this country very closely to the United States. Down the centuries millions of Irish people crossed the Atlantic in search of a new life in a new world. And that tradition of emigration laid the foundation for the strong social, economic and political ties between our two countries today.

Geography has placed this country on the edge of the European continent. One of our most significant achievements as an independent nation was our entry, almost 30 years ago, into what is now the European Union. Today, we have strong social, economic and political ties with the EU.

'Spiritually we are probably a lot closer to Boston than Berlin.'

As Irish people our relationships with the United States and the European Union are complex. Geographically we are closer to Berlin than Boston. Spiritually we are probably a lot closer to Boston than Berlin.

Ireland is now in a very real sense the gateway to Europe. This is especially true for corporate America, whose companies are investing here in ever greater numbers and in ever greater volumes. They see Ireland as an ideal base from which to attack the European market, the largest and most lucrative single market in the history of the world.

Geographic location is not the key factor which influences these corporate decisions: many other places have probably more to offer if that was the deciding issue.

What really makes Ireland attractive to corporate America is the kind of economy which we have created here. When Americans come here they find a country that believes in the incentive power of low taxation. They find a country that believes in economic liberalization. They find a country that believes in essential regulation but not over-regulation. On looking further afield in Europe they find also that not every European country believes in all of these things.

The figures speak for themselves. It is a remarkable fact that a country with just one per cent of Europe's population accounts for 27 per cent of US greenfield investment in Europe.

Political and economic commentators sometimes pose a choice between what they see as the American way and the European way.

They view the American way as being built on the rugged individualism of the original frontiersmen, an economic model that is heavily based on enterprise and incentive, on individual effort and with limited government intervention.

They view the European way as being built on a strong concern for social harmony and social inclusion, with governments being prepared to intervene strongly through the tax and regulatory systems to achieve their desired outcomes.

Both models are, of course, overly simplistic but there is an element of truth in them too. We in Ireland have tended to steer a course between the two but I think it is fair to say that we have sailed closer to the American shore than the European one.

'Ireland is now the fastest-growing country in the developed world.'

Look at what we have done over the last ten years. We have cut taxes on capital. We have cut taxes on corporate profits. We have cut taxes on personal incomes. The result has been an explosion in economic activity and Ireland is now the fastest-growing country in the developed world.

And did we have to pay some very high price for pursuing this policy option? Did we have to dismantle the welfare state? Did we have to abandon the concept of social inclusion? The answer is no: we didn't.

The present government took office three years ago with a clear tax-cutting agenda. Three years on we have increased the number of people at work in this country by 270,000: that's an increase of 20 per cent in 36 months. Over the same period we have brought down the unemployment rate from more than ten per cent to under five per cent. And we have provided very significant real increases in expenditure on key social services such as health, education and training.

We have succeeded because even though we are members of the European Union, including now a currency union also, we still retain very substantial freedom to control our political and economic destiny. Our taxation policy, for instance, is decided in Dublin not Brussels.

This model works. It allows us to achieve our full economic potential for the first time in our history as an independent state. It allows every other member state the freedom to chart its own course for social and economic progress.

'Europe is not America and it never will be.'

And I say: if it ain't broke, don't fix it. There are some who want to create a more centralized Europe, a federal Europe, with key political economic decisions being taken at Brussels level. I don't think that that would be in Ireland's interests and I don't think it would be in Europe's interests either.

The fact is that Europe is not America and it never will be. The people of Europe are not united by common language, common history and common tradition in the way that Americans are. During the next five years, for instance, the process of enlargement is likely to add a further half-a-dozen working languages to the European Union.

It is clear that there is such a thing as a single market for labour in America. Even with the advent of the single currency it is by no means clear that there is a single market for labour in Europe, or that one is likely to emerge anytime soon.

I believe in a Europe of independent states, not a United States of Europe.

'*Ansbacher man.*'

Joe Higgins
(b.1949)

Speech to Dáil Éireann, 11 July 2002

'Ansbacher man.'

All families have their problems, but few have them aired as publicly as the Dunnes. In February 1992, news broke that Ben Dunne, chairman of popular retail chain Dunnes Stores, had been arrested in Florida. High on cocaine, Dunne had threatened to throw himself down the stairwell of a hotel. His public disgrace had a domino effect on Irish politics that few would have foreseen.

Events in Florida prompted a coup by Dunne's siblings to unseat him from the family business. In the process, accountants for the Dunnes Stores Group discovered that Ben had made sizeable payments to politicians. The family dispute was settled privately, but the political donations eventually became a national scandal. In November 1995 allegations were made that the Fine Gael minister for transport, energy and communications, Michael Lowry, had received £200,000 from Dunnes Stores. Further accusations later surfaced that a retired Fianna Fáil politician, rumoured to be former taoiseach Charles Haughey, had received around £1 million.

A tribunal of inquiry was established under Mr Justice Brian McCracken. It lifted the lid on the dodgy world of high finance in Ireland. A picture emerged of private banks and offshore trusts that catered for those who had grown rich during the economic development of the 1960s. The key figure in the tribunal's findings was Des Traynor. The chairman of Cement Roadstone Holdings (CRH), one of Ireland's most profitable companies, had established the Cayman Bank in the early 1970s. Traynor had effectively run this offshore bank (later sold to the Ansbacher group) from a CRH office in Dublin. Tánaiste Mary Harney ordered an inquiry into Ansbacher, which reinforced a picture of murky offshore finance. Public opinion was scandalized that during the bitter years of depression in the 1980s, 'fat cat' businessmen had still been getting the cream while the rest of the country suffered.

BIOGRAPHY

Joe Higgins was born in Lispole, County Kerry, in 1949 and grew up on a small farm with eight siblings. He went to the United States to train for the priesthood, but he left the seminary after being radicalized by the civil rights movement and anti-Vietnam protests. After returning to Ireland, Higgins, a member of the Trotskyite Militant tendency, joined the Labour Party. When Militant was expelled from the party in 1989, Higgins went with it and eventually established his own Socialist Party. Elected to Dáil Éireann in 1997, he served for ten years as the party's only TD. He lost his seat at the 2007 general election.

Joe Higgins might have been the one and only Socialist Party deputy in Dáil Éireann, but most recognized that in this contemptuous statement on 11 July 2002 about the Ansbacher report, he spoke for the nation.

The inspectors appointed to inquire into the affairs of Ansbacher (Cayman) Limited have thrown a remarkable light on the twilight world of a subspecies of humanity which wielded enormous power and influence in Irish business and politics.

Previously, I called this species 'Ansbacher man'. Ansbacher man was brought into being in the 1970s. Like his creator, he had a complex, dual personality, one half of which was 'Ansbacher man the shadow', a shadowy persona who inhabited a secret world of offshore islands, coded bank deposits, fiddled taxes and secret loans.

'Ansbacher man the shadow was as furtive as a thief.'

Leaving his plush boardroom or magnificent suburban mansion, he flitted in and out of the lobbies of top hotels, restaurants, clubs and pubs to rendezvous with his creator who handed him or took from him as the case may be bulky packages of tax-evading cash or more discreet cheques or bank drafts. Ansbacher man the shadow was as furtive as a thief. He was driven by greed and the inordinate desire for personal enrichment. He was a walking conspiracy to defraud the taxation system of tens of millions, if not hundreds of millions, of pounds.

Meanwhile, his other half, 'Ansbacher man the public persona', was generally basking in the warm glow of an approving establishment. Business colleagues, priests and political party leaders all deferred to him and his picture was in the business pages of the *Irish Times* every second day. He was on high-powered committees which laid down industrial policy for this country for years and decades to come. He was enthusiastic about pouring millions of pounds of taxpayers' money – PAYE taxpayers' money – into subventions for industry, just as he was unenthusiastic about industry being obliged to return the compliment to the PAYE taxpayer.

In the 1980s he was forthright in calling on the unemployed and the crucified, compliant PAYE taxpayer alike to tighten their belts in the national interest. He regretted the relentless rise in unemployment and the stream of talented youth forced to emigrate. He wrung his hands as hospital beds were closed by the hundred, if not the thousand, mentally ill people were sent in to communities which had not been prepared for them and the old and sick waited in pain for medical procedures that never materialized because the taxes were not there to pay for them – Ansbacher man the shadow had already salted them away in the Caribbean islands, far from Blanchardstown, Clondalkin, Knocknaheeny and Fairhill. Between the two worlds of Ansbacher man stood his creator. A cross between an octopus and Spiderman, Mr Traynor's tentacles reached into very many corners while his web encompassed very many people in business and politics at the very top of society.

Then disaster struck. Appropriately it began with one of his own standing at the top of a stairwell in a Florida hotel threatening to throw himself down. I am sure many of the unmasked Ansbacher account holders rue the fact that they were not present to shout 'Jump, Ben, jump, it will not hurt.'

The McCracken report unmasked the secret world of Ansbacher man, revealing for all to see the corruption at the heart of crony capitalism, masquerading as a political and business establishment. The same establishment wants to say 'that was then, this is now.' The tánaiste hinted at this in her speech. We are told that Ansbacher man is as extinct as Neanderthal man or the Tuatha De Danann and that to believe otherwise is as foolish as to say that fairies inhabit the *liosanna* and *ráthanna* they left behind. The establishment is trying to make us believe that Ansbacher man was an aberration, a branch of evolution that suddenly ended and has disappeared without trace, but that is not the case. Ansbacher man as we came to know him is extinct, but his DNA lives on. His genetic fingerprint can be found at the heart of major business conglomerates in this state … capitalism is built on greed. Corruption is endemic in the capitalist system. I want to see that system replaced with a society that is truly democratic and free from corruption, where wealth is possessed by working people and where there is no incentive to be corrupt. That is the system of democratic socialism I favour. We have to insist on immediate measures to root out the corruption that doubtless remains.

'We have to insist on immediate measures to root out the corruption that doubtless remains.'

What now for the Ansbacher clients? It was fascinating to dip into the interviews they had with the inspectors. One might be forgiven when reading such interviews for thinking that one had stumbled upon transcripts of proceedings in the offices of the Irish Association for Victim Support. We are almost led to believe that Mr Traynor mugged these people and that they are nothing more than injured innocents. We are supposed to believe that weapons of charm, reassurance and bonhomie were used to separate them from their money, which then somehow ended up in offshore accounts.

My party seeks the prosecution of all those engaged in the Ansbacher conspiracy to defraud. Their assets should be seized and applied to the public services that suffered. Although I do not dispute that prison sentences would be in order, a few years of community service at the coalface may be more appropriate so that those who engaged in fraud might, for the first time, encounter the society in which real people live …

'I will introduce a prohibition
on smoking.'

Mícheál Martin
(b.1960)

Speech in Dublin, 30 January 2003

'I will introduce a prohibition on smoking.'

Mícheál Martin, the Fianna Fáil minister for health and children, had attempted to ban cigarette advertising in 2002. The tobacco industry hit back with legal action that ended in Martin's provisions being struck down by the high court. Faced with the option of 'stick or twist', Martin decided to risk all in facing down this powerful lobby group. On 30 January 2003, following publication of Health Effects of Environmental Tobacco Smoke in the Workplace, the minister announced his intention to ban smoking in all places of employment. Uproar ensued. The debate focused on pubs and restaurants. Tobacco- and alcohol-vested interests threatened more legal action and lobbied to scrap the proposals in favour of ventilation systems to purify the air in pubs. A host of Fianna Fáil backbenchers opposed the ban. The minister, however, was having none of it. 'I'm happy I am doing the right thing for the Irish people,' he said defiantly on the *Late Late Show*. 'I'm also satisfied that generations to come will look back and say this was the right decision.'

In facing down opposition, Mícheál Martin spoke for public opinion. Polls consistently showed that two out of three people supported the measure. Even 40 per cent of smokers were in favour. Martin announced that a ban in all workplaces (except prisons and psychiatric hospitals) would take effect on 1 January 2004. In a clever move, he delayed implementation until late March, when the weather was a little more clement for the smoking community huddling outside pubs, cafés and offices across the country.

Ireland was the first European country to introduce a national smoking ban. The measure attracted worldwide coverage, much of it amazed that the Irish were giving up the *craic* of smoke-filled bars. Most ordinary punters, however, agreed that Ireland overnight became a more enjoyable place in which to live and drink. And the ban gave life to the new phenomenon of smirting – smoking and flirting – among those nipping outside for a quick puff.

While the tobacco industry has played down any possibility of danger in passive smoking, the advice contained in this report is blunt. Current ventilation technologies are inadequate to give workers full protection from the hazards of tobacco smoke. Exposure can best be controlled by banning smoking in places of work. Acting on this advice I will introduce a prohibition on

BIOGRAPHY

Mícheál Martin was born in Cork in 1960, the son of an international boxer, and was educated at University College, Cork. He was elected to Dáil Éireann in 1989 and in 1997 became (at 36) the youngest cabinet member of the first Ahern administration. He served successively as minister for education, for health, and for enterprise, trade and employment. During the 2007 election campaign, he took a highly visible role in defending Bertie Ahern at the height of the crisis over the taoiseach's personal financial affairs. Martin was reappointed as minister for enterprise, trade and employment in the third Ahern administration.

smoking tobacco products in places of work and I have today published draft regulations providing for this. Following a consultation period, I intend to introduce these regulations on 1 January 2004.

The World Health Organization's International Agency for Research on Cancer has recently declared, without equivocation, that environmental tobacco smoke is carcinogenic to humans and it includes more than 50 known carcinogens – frightening when one realizes that these are being inhaled for prolonged periods by many non-smokers every day. The bottom line is you don't have to be a smoker to get cancer from cigarette smoking. You can get it if you were never a smoker. That declaration, together with the increasing concern about the health effects of environmental tobacco smoke, led to this report.

As children grow, exposure to environmental tobacco smoke significantly reduces their lung capacity and exercise tolerance. It damages the health of children right from the start: for example, it lowers birth weight. It has been identified as a cause of asthma attacks and middle ear disease.

'There is a growing demand for increased protection from environmental tobacco smoke.'

Almost 70 per cent of the adult population in Ireland are non-smokers yet many people are unwillingly exposed, on a daily basis, to toxic environmental tobacco smoke. Many public areas and facilities and some workplaces are subject to prohibitions and restrictions on smoking and there is a growing demand for increased protection from environmental tobacco smoke. Opinion polls here show there is enormous public support, almost 90 per cent, for extending bans on environmental tobacco smoke. Even many smokers are supportive of prohibitions on smoking in public places. Optimal protection for non-smokers and smokers is best provided by smoke-free areas. Workers' representatives have been concerned for some time over the threat to the health of employees from toxic tobacco smoke. I have spoken to representatives of the trade union movement on this matter and I appreciate their support for wide-ranging measures to eliminate tobacco smoke in the workplace. It is only fair that we have a 'level playing field' in this important area of public health and that the health of workers is protected on an equitable basis for all.

For far too long in Ireland, we've had the habit of shrugging our shoulders about health, as if it was something that simply happened. Removing tobacco damage from our lives will have a long-term and significant positive effect on our health as well as on domestic and workplace well-being. This government is going to act on this report and deliver those entitlements.

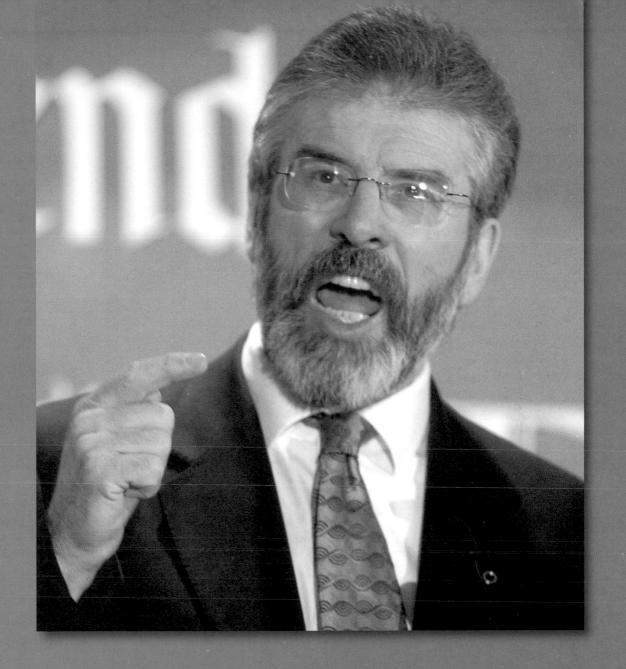

'*Now there is an alternative.*'

Gerry Adams
(b.1948)

Speech in Belfast, 6 April 2005

The Northern Ireland Assembly, established under the terms of the Belfast Agreement, was suspended in October 2002 amid accusations of a republican spy ring in Stormont and counter-accusations of dirty tricks by British intelligence.

Though the IRA had begun decommissioning the previous year, the suggestion that it was still actively engaged in intelligence gathering raised obvious concerns. Moreover, the continued involvement of paramilitaries in criminal rackets and local 'policing' – for example, knee-capping those involved in 'anti-social behaviour' – made it obvious that, in the words of Gerry Adams, 'they haven't gone away, you know.'

Security forces in both jurisdictions had largely been willing to turn a blind eye to facilitate the continuing ceasefire. Late in 2004, however, the IRA seemed to go a step too far. On 20 December, it was alleged to have masterminded a bank raid that netted £26.5 million, the biggest ever such robbery in Britain or Ireland. More than the act itself, the heist raised the question what the IRA might be planning to do with the money. Months of political and media condemnation followed. The IRA response came on 2 February 2005: a withdrawal of the offer to put weapons 'beyond use'.

The bank raid had proved damaging both to the IRA and Sinn Féin. Even more detrimental was the murder of a Belfast man, Robert McCartney, in a brawl outside a pub in the Short Strand area. A number of senior republicans were known to have been present, but the resulting police investigation met with a wall of silence. This prompted McCartney's fiancée and sisters to begin a campaign to bring his killers to justice. The IRA eventually held its own inquiry and expelled three members. On 7 March, it offered to 'shoot' those responsible (a proposal the McCartney sisters rejected). The IRA's offer of rough justice did little to improve its international standing. The traditional St Patrick's day invitation from the White House that year went to the McCartney family rather than Gerry Adams.

Out in the political cold, and facing local and Westminster elections, Sinn Féin needed to draw a line under recent events. On 6 April 2005, Adams made this unambiguous call on the IRA to engage solely in democratic activity. Three months later, the IRA announced that it would support the political process.

BIOGRAPHY

Gerry Adams was born into a working-class family in west Belfast in 1948, the oldest child of ten. He left school at 17 and joined Sinn Féin the following year. This led him into what he termed 'defence work' in Catholic areas of west Belfast following the outbreak of civil unrest in 1969. From this time onwards, the security forces stated that he was a member of the IRA, a charge he has always denied. Adams was instrumental in shaping Sinn Féin's 'armalite and ballot box' strategy from 1981. Over the next quarter of a century, that policy would see Sinn Féin established as the majority party representing Northern Ireland's nationalist community. He continues as president of the party, but has not taken government office.

'Now there is an alternative.'

I want to speak directly to the men and women of Óglaigh na hÉireann, the volunteer soldiers of the Irish Republican Army. In time of great peril you stepped into the Bearna Baoil, the gap of danger. When others stood idly by, you and your families gave your all, in defence of a risen people and in pursuit of Irish freedom and unity. Against mighty odds you held the line and faced down a huge military foe, the British Crown forces and their surrogates in the unionist death squads … For over 30 years, the IRA showed that the British government could not rule Ireland on its own terms. You asserted the legitimacy of the right of the people of this island to freedom and independence. Many of your comrades made the ultimate sacrifice. Your determination, selflessness and courage have brought the freedom struggle towards its fulfilment. That struggle can now be taken forward by other means. I say this with the authority of my office as president of Sinn Féin.

'Can you take courageous initiatives which will achieve your aims by purely political and democratic activity?'

In the past I have defended the right of the IRA to engage in armed struggle. I did so because there was no alternative for those who would not bend the knee, or turn a blind eye to oppression, or for those who wanted a national republic.

Now there is an alternative.

I have clearly set out my view of what that alternative is. The way forward is by building political support for republican and democratic objectives across Ireland and by winning support for these goals internationally.

I want to use this occasion therefore to appeal to the leadership of Óglaigh na hÉireann to fully embrace and accept this alternative.

Can you take courageous initiatives which will achieve your aims by purely political and democratic activity?

I know full well that such truly historic decisions can only be taken in the aftermath of intense internal consultation. I ask that you initiate this as quickly as possible.

'Republicans need to lead by example.'

I understand fully that the IRA's most recent positive contribution to the peace process was in the context of a comprehensive agreement. But I also hold the very strong view that republicans need to lead by example. There is no greater demonstration of this than the IRA cessation in the summer of 1994.

Sinn Féin has demonstrated the ability to play a leadership role as part of a popular movement towards peace, equality and justice. We are totally committed to ending partition and to creating the conditions for unity and independence. Sinn Féin has the potential and capacity to become the vehicle for the attainment of republican objectives.

The Ireland we live in today is also a very different place from 15 years ago. There is now an all-Ireland agenda with huge potential. Nationalists and republicans have a confidence that will never again allow anyone to be treated as second-class citizens. Equality is our watchword. The catalyst for much of this change is the growing support for republicanism.

Of course, those who oppose change are not going to simply roll over. It will always be a battle a day between those who want maximum change and those who want to maintain the *status quo*.

But if republicans are to prevail, if the peace process is to be successfully concluded and Irish sovereignty and reunification secured, then we have to set the agenda – no one else is going to do that.

So, I also want to make a personal appeal to all of you – the women and men volunteers who have remained undefeated in the face of tremendous odds. Now is the time for you to step into the Bearna Baoil again; not as volunteers risking life and limb but as activists in a national movement towards independence and unity.

'Our struggle has reached a defining moment.'

Such decisions will be far-reaching and difficult. But you never lacked courage in the past. Your courage is now needed for the future. It won't be easy. There are many problems to be resolved by the people of Ireland in the time ahead. Your ability as republican volunteers to rise to this challenge will mean that the two governments and others cannot easily hide from their obligations and their responsibility to resolve these problems.

Our struggle has reached a defining moment.

I am asking you to join me in seizing this moment, to intensify our efforts, to rebuild the peace process and decisively move our struggle forward.

'Their deaths rise far above
the clamour.'

Mary McAleese
(b.1951)

Speech at University College, Cork, 27 January 2006

When it came to the disputed legacy of 1916, context was often everything. In the setting of the 'troubles', some revisionist historians and the liberal media were keen to portray the Easter Rising as the insurrection of a bloodthirsty, anti-democratic, lunatic cabal that had established the template for the Provisional IRA. Traditional republicans they accused of adhering to 'narrow nationalism'. The annual military parade past the GPO was a particular target for denigration. Critics said that in glorifying violence and revolution, it legitimized the campaign of the IRA. In 1970, the Fianna Fáil government quietly scrapped the march.

By 2006 the Northern Ireland peace process had transformed the political landscape. Ceasefires and paramilitary decommissioning meant that the legacy of the Rising seemed less problematic than three decades earlier. Moreover, Sinn Féin's electoral popularity was on the rise, and the traditional mainstream parties were looking for ways to assert their own 1916 credentials. In October 2005, the taoiseach, Bertie Ahern, told delegates at the Fianna Fáil Ard Fheis that the government planned to restore the military parade. 'The Irish people need to reclaim the spirit of 1916,' he declared, 'which is not the property of those who have abused and debased the title of republicanism.'

The decision to hold the parade opened the floodgates of commemoration. On 27 January 2006, President Mary McAleese launched a conference at University College, Cork, on the Rising with an unapologetically nationalist address. Opponents had often tried to exploit her Northern Ireland upbringing. This unreconstructed speech threw that criticism back in their faces. She concluded by mischievously encouraging delegates to 'enjoy the conference and the rows it will surely rise'.

None was fiercer than that surrounding her own contribution. The speech met with a barrage of criticism. Kevin Myers fumed in the *Irish Times* that the President's 'wretched ... triumphalist address' probably ranked 'as among the most imbecilic ever, by any president, ever'. Yet Mary McAleese had undoubtedly spoken for many, perhaps the majority, in Ireland; certainly the attendance of some 120,000 people in Dublin for the military parade on Easter Sunday that year suggested that she was not alone.

BIOGRAPHY

Mary McAleese was born in Belfast in 1951, the eldest of nine children. Her early life was scarred by the 'troubles' – the family ran a famous pub in the Falls Road area of west Belfast but was forced to leave when sectarian violence broke out in the early 1970s. A prominent lawyer and academic, she was elected on a Fianna Fáil ticket as president of Ireland in 1997 and was returned uncontested seven years later. President McAleese was the first holder of the office from Northern Ireland. A popular president, she has nevertheless not been afraid to raise sensitive issues and even court controversy, not least when she (a Catholic) took communion at the Anglican cathedral of Christ Church, Dublin in 1997.

'Their deaths rise far above the clamour.'

How glad I am that I was not the mother of adult children in January 1916. Would my 20-year-old son and his friends be among the tens of thousands in British uniform heading for the Somme or would they be among the few, training in secret with the Irish Republican Brotherhood, or with the Irish Volunteers? Would I, like so many mothers, bury my son this fateful year in some army's uniform, in a formidably unequal country where I have no vote or voice, where many young men are destined to be cannon fodder, and women, widows? How many times did those men and women wonder what the world would be like in the longer run as a result of the outworking of the chaos around them, this context we struggle to comprehend these years later? I am grateful that I, and my children, live in the longer run; for while we could speculate endlessly about what life might be like if the Rising had not happened, or if the Great War had not been fought, we who live in these times know and inhabit the world that revealed itself because they happened...

'A widely shared political philosophy of equality and social inclusion.'

With each passing year, post-Rising Ireland reveals itself and we, who are of this strong independent and high-achieving Ireland, would do well to ponder the extent to which today's freedoms, values, ambitions and success rest on that perilous and militarily doomed undertaking of nine decades ago, and on the words of that Proclamation. Clearly its fundamental idea was freedom, or in the words of the Proclamation, 'the right of the Irish people to the ownership of Ireland', but it was also a very radical assertion of the kind of republic a liberated Ireland should become. 'The Republic guarantees religious and civil liberty, equal rights and equal opportunities to all its citizens and declares its resolve to pursue the happiness and prosperity of the whole nation and all of its parts cherishing all of the children of the nation equally ...' It spoke of a Parliament 'representative of the whole people of Ireland and elected by the suffrages of all her men and women' – this at a time when Westminster was still refusing to concede the vote to women on the basis that to do so would be to give in to terrorism. To our 21st-century ears these words seem a good fit for our modern democracy. Yet 90 years ago, even 40 years ago, they seemed hopelessly naïve, and their long-term intellectual power was destined to be overlooked, as interest was focused on the emotionally charged political power of the Rising and the renewed nationalist fervour it evoked.

In the longer term the apparent naïveté of the words of the Proclamation has filled out into a widely shared political philosophy of equality and social inclusion in tune with the contemporary spirit of democracy, human rights, equality and anti-confessionalism. Read now in the light of the liberation of women, the development of social partnership, the focus on rights and equality, the ending of the special position of the Catholic church to mention but a few, we see a much more coherent, and wider reaching, intellectual event than may have previously been noted.

The kind of Ireland the heroes of the Rising aspired to was based on an inclusivity that, famously, would 'cherish all the children of the nation equally – oblivious of the differences which have divided a minority from the majority in the past'. That culture of inclusion is manifestly a strong contemporary impulse working its way today through relationships with the North, with unionists, with the newcomers to our shores, with our marginalized, and with our own increasing diversity …

'The kind of Ireland the heroes of the Rising aspired to.'

There is a tendency for powerful and pitiless elites to dismiss with damning labels those who oppose them. That was probably the source of the accusation that 1916 was an exclusive and sectarian enterprise. It was never that, though ironically it was an accurate description of what the Rising opposed.

In 1916, Ireland was a small nation attempting to gain its independence from one of Europe's many powerful empires. In the 19th century an English radical described the occupation of India as a system of 'outdoor relief' for the younger sons of the upper classes. The administration of Ireland was not very different, being carried on as a process of continuous conversation around the fire in the Kildare Street Club by past pupils of public schools. It was no way to run a country …

The leaders of the Rising … were not attempting to establish an isolated and segregated territory of 'ourselves alone', as the phrase *sinn féin* is so often mistranslated, but a free country in which we ourselves could take responsibility for our own destiny, a country that could stand up for itself, have its own distinct perspective, pull itself up by its bootstraps, and be counted with respect, among the free nations of Europe and the world.

A google search for the phrase 'narrow nationalism' produces about 28,000 results. It is almost as though some people cannot use the word 'nationalism' without qualifying it by the word 'narrow'. But that does not make it correct.

'Irish nationalism, from the start, was a multilateral enterprise.'

I have a strong impression that to its enemies, both in Ireland and abroad, Irish nationalism looked like a version of the imperialism it opposed, a sort of 'imperialism lite' through which Ireland would attempt to be what the Great European powers were – the domination of one cultural and ethnic tradition over others. It is easy to see how they might have fallen into that mistaken view, but mistaken they were. Irish nationalism, from the start, was a multilateral enterprise, attempting to escape the dominance of a single class and, in our case, a largely foreign class, into a wider world. Those who think of Irish nationalists as narrow, miss, for example, the membership many of them had of a universal church which brought them into contact with a vastly wider segment of the world than that open to even the most travelled imperial English gentleman. Many of the leaders had experience of the Americas, and in particular of North America with its vibrant attachment to liberty and democracy. Others of them were active participants in the international working-class movements of their day. Whatever you might think of those involvements, they were universalist and global rather than constricted and blinkered …

Paradoxically, in the longer run, 1916 arguably set in motion a calming of old conflicts with new concepts and confidence which, as they mature and take shape, stand us is in good stead today … This year, the 90th anniversary of the 1916 Rising, and of the Somme, has the potential to be a pivotal year for peace and reconcili-ation, to be a time of shared pride for the divided grandchildren of those who died, whether at Messines or in Kilmainham …

'We are where freedom has brought us.'

In the hearts of those who took part in the Rising, in what was then an undivided Ireland, was an unshakeable belief that whatever our personal political or religious perspectives, there was huge potential for an Ireland in which loyalist, republican, unionist, nationalist, Catholic, Protestant, atheist, agnostic pulled together to build a shared future, owned by one and all. That's a longer term to conjure with but, for now, reflecting back on the sacrifices of the heroes of 1916 and the gallingly unjust world that was their context, I look at my own context and its threads of connection to theirs. I am humbled, excited and grateful to live in one of the world's most respected, admired and successful democracies, a country with an identifiably distinctive voice in Europe and in the world, an Irish republic, a sovereign independent state to use the words of the Proclamation. We are where freedom has brought us. A tough journey, but more than vindicated by our contemporary context. Like every nation that had to wrench its freedom from the reluctant grip of empire we have our idealistic and heroic founding fathers and mothers, our Davids to their Goliaths. That small band who proclaimed the Rising inhabited a sea of death, an unspeakable time of the most profligate worldwide waste of human life. Yet their deaths rise far above the clamour – their voices insistent still.

Enjoy the conference and the rows it will surely rise. *Slán libh.*

'Ireland needs to cherish its roots.'

Bertie Ahern

(b.1951)

Speech at Dublin Castle, 26 February 2007

The 'Mother and Child' crisis in 1951 marked the zenith of church influence in independent Ireland, but it was a Pyrrhic victory. Even many Catholics condemned the hierarchy for overstepping the mark. Afterwards the bishops became more circumspect and, as the decades passed, so their influence began to fade. A constitutional referendum in 1972 removed the clause acknowledging the 'special position' of the church, which had been a longstanding grievance for Protestants in Northern Ireland. Liberal reforms on contraception, gay rights and divorce were introduced in the 1980s and 1990s. Revelations about the hierarchy's failure to deal with generations of clerical sexual abuse saw their moral authority collapse almost beyond repair.

In July 2005 Bertie Ahern announced, as part of an EU-wide process, the establishment of structures for formal dialogue between the government and the faiths operating within the state. Although many libertarians and secularists regarded this as a controversial development, the decision to bring discussion into the open was broadly welcomed. Moreover, in the context of increased national and religious diversity in Ireland, and the worldwide problems arising from growing fundamentalism, it seemed more necessary than ever to engage in a discourse on faith and society.

The taoiseach's speech on 26 February 2007 to inaugurate 'structured dialogue' touched on all these points, but also went beyond them. He expressed an unease that the nation, having transformed itself into the 'Celtic tiger', was in danger of losing its soul. 'A fast-changing Ireland … needs to cherish its roots,' Ahern warned. 'Turning our back as a country on our living and vibrant life of religious faith would be a loss and would be a mistake.' In particular, while acknowledging the dark 'shadow' of child abuse, he spoke forcefully about the need to remember the role of the churches in 'the building up of this country and its place in the world'.

The *Irish Times* commentator John Waters described Ahern's address as 'the most interesting speech by a politician for years'.

BIOGRAPHY

Bertie Ahern was born in Drumcondra in 1951, the son of a veteran of the war of independence who took the anti-Treaty side during the civil war. He was first elected to Dáil Éireann in 1977 and subsequently succeeded Albert Reynolds as the leader of Fianna Fáil in 1994. He won general elections in 1997, 2002 and 2007, with success in each being widely attributed by political commentators to the 'Bertie factor'. His two daughters also live in the public eye: Cecelia is the international bestselling author of books that include *PS, I Love You*; Georgina is married to Nicky Byrne of the band Westlife.

... Ireland shares in the inheritance of over 2000 years of Christianity. This heritage has indelibly shaped our country, our culture and our course for the future. We are home too, to people of other faiths and it is a special feature of the past decade that we have welcomed what, in a historical context, are relatively large numbers of non-Christian people.

'Ireland needs to cherish its roots, if our society is to mature and to flourish.'

A fast-changing Ireland needs not only to adapt and to move on. It needs to cherish its roots, if our society is to mature and to flourish...

That governments cannot legislate for morality is an old and true saying. The government of this republic is not and must not be sectarian. It is not our role to promote, or to actively protect the role or position of any church or faith.

What we can do, however, is be open and attentive to the views, the attitudes and the valuable contribution of all our religious communities to the ongoing life and future direction of the nation. Ireland at the beginning of the 21st century did not arrive ready made, with a set of views and attitudes, in a vacuum-packed container. Our country, our strengths and our weaknesses are all part of a long gestation of history, of culture and of religious belief. We cannot understand who we are today, let alone where we hope to go tomorrow, if we do not first understand and listen with an open ear to the deepest influences within our national life.

A further consideration in initiating this process is the recognition of the contribution which the churches and church personnel have made to the building up of this country and its place in the world.

Wherever in the world Irish representatives travel, we find direct evidence of the extent to which Irish men and women of all Christian traditions have been inspired by the Gospel to find new homes and new communities, far from their place of birth.

They have contributed much to the building up of nations across the globe. They have created a powerfully positive image for our country and its people, far beyond the impact our population would suggest.

At home, it is to many visionary church personnel, from all the denominations on the island, that we owe particular thanks for facilitating our education as a people. It is they who recognized the importance of education for life. Thanks to those men and women, many gifted children from less privileged backgrounds were able to realize their full potential in life. At a time when the expectations and opportunities for young women in Ireland were extraordinarily limited, religious sisters were the loudest, and sometimes the only, champions of education for girls. This contribution endures, despite the shadow cast by other, more painful events.

'The government is also anxious to develop its relationship with the non-Christian traditions.'

Embarking on this initiative, the government is also anxious to develop its relationship with the non-Christian traditions. The Jewish community has been present in Ireland for many centuries and has played a very substantial part in the commercial, cultural and political life of Irish society. The community has provided personalities who have made a profound contribution through their leadership in their chosen field of activity. As a Dubliner, I am acutely conscious of the distinctive role of the Jewish community in this city. Indeed, the very image of the modern Dubliner has, thanks to Joyce, been forever associated with the inheritance of its Jewish community. It is a matter of great concern that the characteristically 'Irish' Jewish community should continue and thrive.

Recent patterns of migration very substantially increased the size of the Islamic community in Ireland. Their presence here has enriched the cultural life of our society. The pattern of events at a global level have underlined the importance of developing better knowledge, closer relations and a climate of inclusion and respect as this growing community develops its place within Irish society. It requires us, for example, to recall and appreciate the contribution which Islamic scholars and leaders made to the European inheritance, in philosophy, the sciences and literature. We do well also to recall that large Islamic populations have lived in parts of Europe for very many centuries and are an intrinsic part of the European experience.

We would do well to recognize that the churches and faith communities can be, in themselves, a powerful means to help those who migrate to this country to feel at home and to be confident in their new environment. This is most likely when their churches and faith communities are themselves confident of their place of respect in Irish civil society.

There are some who feel that the modern era is one with a shrinking role for religion, religious belief and religious identity. Our own experience over recent years demonstrates that this is not the case. On the contrary, so much of what is happening within our society and in the wider world is bound up with questions of religion, religious identity and religious belief, that governments which refuse or fail to engage with religious communities and religious identities risk failing in their fundamental duties to their citizens.

'Illiberal voices would diminish our democracy.'

There is a form of aggressive secularism which would have the state and state institutions ignore the importance of this religious dimension. They argue that the state and public policy should become intolerant of religious belief and preference, and confine it, at best, to the purely private and personal, without rights or a role within the public domain. Such illiberal voices would diminish our democracy. They would deny a crucial dimension of the dignity of every person and their rights to live out their spiritual code within a framework of lawful practice, which is respectful of the dignity and rights of all citizens. It would be a betrayal of the best traditions of Irish Republicanism to create such an environment…

I believe that all issues of mutual interest and concern can, in principle, be covered by structured dialogue. This process will not displace the well-established lines of communication between churches and church-based organizations on specific issues of concern to them, such as the administration and funding of services. Any dialogue of this kind must, of course, be transparent and open.

Rather, these opportunities for enhanced dialogue should relate to issues of faith itself and the role of the churches in society, on the one hand, and their views on major social and policy issues, on the other.

We live in a pluralist society, where doubt and disbelief exist side by side with an increasing diversity of faiths. But it is also a time of hope; a hope born of the vibrant traditions of our people and of the ultimate vision which has inspired men and women of faith over many generations.

'We live in a pluralist society.'

There is hope, too, in the recognition that embracing difference and diversity can intensify and deepen self-understanding. As I have said before, the state is not indifferent. It is a willing partner with the churches, a grateful beneficiary of the cultural and spiritual efforts of communities of faith, and a supporter of the search for reconciled and harmonious diversity among the churches and faith communities.

As a society and as a government, we treasure the spiritual, and we respect the prophetic role of spiritual leaders …

I believe that we are today putting in place a process which will build up a more tolerant, inclusive, reflective society, which will continue to change and evolve but which, like all societies over time, will continue the search for the meaning of life, the basis for the living of a good life, and the means to live in peace and harmony with our neighbours.

'Northern Ireland has come
to a time of peace.'

Ian Paisley
(b.1926)

Speech at Stormont, 8 May 2007

Though the Belfast Agreement and paramilitary ceasefires had brought an end to the worst violence in Northern Ireland, the years that followed saw politics polarize. Sinn Féin and the Democratic Unionist Party (DUP) eclipsed the Ulster Unionists and the SDLP. With the DUP vehemently opposed to power-sharing with Sinn Féin, the impasse to restoring the Stormont assembly looked all but unbreakable.

Without any expectation of progress, the Blair administration decided to focus minds with a carrot and stick approach. The secretary of state for Northern Ireland, Peter Hain, announced that if politicians could not come to an agreement about power-sharing by 26 March 2007, then devolution would end and direct rule from Westminster would be permanently restored. Northern Ireland could then expect to see the introduction of unpopular measures such as water charges. On the other hand, if the parties could agree, the government promised a £50 billion investment package for the province over ten years. It was an offer that was difficult to refuse.

On the morning of the deadline, Ian Paisley and Gerry Adams announced at a press conference that they had agreed to share power in a devolved government from May onwards. It was the first ever face-to-face meeting of the two; Paisley had previously refused even to meet with representatives of the party he had always referred to as Sinn Féin-IRA.

Uncharacteristically for Northern Ireland, there were no last-minute hitches. On 8 May 2007, Ian Paisley was sworn in as first minister alongside Sinn Féin's Martin McGuinness as deputy first minister. It had been a long journey for the founder of the DUP from 'never surrender' to this declaration that 'Northern Ireland has come to a time of peace.' It was a day, said British prime minister Tony Blair, that did 'a power of good for optimists everywhere'.

The 'troubles' had cost some 3722 lives between 11 June 1966 and 8 May 2007.

BIOGRAPHY

Ian Paisley was born in Lurgan, County Armagh in 1926. He took a leading role in forming the Free Presbyterian Church, which provided a platform for his brand of 'bible Protestantism' and unionism. From the 1960s onwards, he was a vociferous critic of accommodation with Irish nationalism, and opposed variously the Sunningdale (1973), Anglo-Irish (1985) and Good Friday (1998) agreements. 'Ian, if the word "no" were to be removed from the English language,' SDLP leader John Hume once told him, 'you'd be speechless, wouldn't you?' ('No, I wouldn't!' Paisley replied). Even during the 2006 marching season he told the Orange Order that Sinn Féin were 'not fit to be in the government of Northern Ireland and it will be over our dead bodies if they ever get there'. Ten months later a very much alive Paisley joined them as first minister in a power-sharing government.

'Northern Ireland has come to a time of peace.'

How true are the words of holy scripture, 'We know not what a day may bring forth.'

If anyone had told me that I would be standing here today to take this office, I would have been totally unbelieving. I am here by the vote of the majority of the electorate of our beloved province.

'But that was yesterday, this is today, and tomorrow is tomorrow.'

During the past few days I have listened to many very well-placed people from outside Northern Ireland seeking to emphasize the contribution they claim to have made in bringing it about.

However, the real truth of the matter is rather different.

If those same people had only allowed the Ulster people to settle the matter without their interference and insistence upon their way and their way alone, we would all have come to this day a lot earlier.

I remember well the night the Belfast Agreement was signed, I was wrongfully arrested and locked up on the orders of the then-secretary of state for Northern Ireland. It was only after the assistant chief of police intervened that I was released. On my release I was kicked and cursed by certain loyalists who supported the Belfast Agreement. But that was yesterday, this is today, and tomorrow is tomorrow.

'We are all aiming to build a Northern Ireland in which all can live together in peace.'

Today at long last we are starting upon the road – I emphasize starting – which I believe will take us to lasting peace in our province. I have not changed my unionism, the Union of Northern Ireland within the United Kingdom, which I believe is today stronger than ever.

We are making this declaration, we are all aiming to build a Northern Ireland in which all can live together in peace, being equal under the law and equally subject to the law.

I welcome the pledge we have all taken to that effect today. That is the rock foundation upon which we must build.

Today we salute Ulster's honoured and unageing dead – the innocent victims, that gallant band, members of both religions, Protestant and Roman Catholic, strong in their allegiance to their differing political beliefs, unionist and nationalist, male and female, children and adults, all innocent victims of the terrible conflict.

In the shadows of the evenings and in the sunrise of the mornings we hail their gallantry and heroism. It cannot and will not be erased from our memories.

Nor can we forget those who continue to bear the scars of suffering and whose bodies have been robbed of sight, robbed of hearing, robbed of limbs. Yes, and we must all shed the silent and bitter tear for those whose loved one's bodies have not yet been returned.

Let me read to you the words of Deirdre Speer, who lost her police officer father in the struggle:

> Remember me! Remember me!
> My sculptured glens where crystal rivers run,
> My purple mountains, misty in the sun,
> My coastlines, little changed since time begun,
> I gave you birth.
> Remember me! Remember me!
> Though battle-scarred and weary I abide.
> When you speak of history say my name with pride.
> I am Ulster.

'I have sensed a great sigh of relief amongst all our people who want the hostility to be replaced with neighbourliness.'

In politics, as in life, it is a truism that no one can ever have 100 per cent of what they desire. They must make a verdict when they believe they have achieved enough to move things forward. Unlike at any other time I believe we are now able to make progress.

Winning support for all the institutions of policing has been a critical test that today has been met in pledged word and deed. Recognizing the significance of that change from a community that for decades demonstrated hostility for policing has been critical in Ulster turning the corner.

I have sensed a great sigh of relief amongst all our people who want the hostility to be replaced with neighbourliness.

'Northern Ireland has come to a time of peace.'

The great king Solomon said:

> To everything there is a season, and a time to every purpose under heaven.
> A time to be born and a time to die.
> A time to plant and a time to pluck up that which is planted.
> A time to kill and a time to heal.
> A time to break down and a time to build up.
> A time to get and a time to lose.
> A time to keep and a time to cast away.
> A time to love and a time to hate.
> A time of war and a time of peace.

'Today we have begun to plant and we await the harvest.'

I believe that Northern Ireland has come to a time of peace, a time when hate will no longer rule.

How good it will be to be part of a wonderful healing in our province.

Today we have begun to plant and we await the harvest.

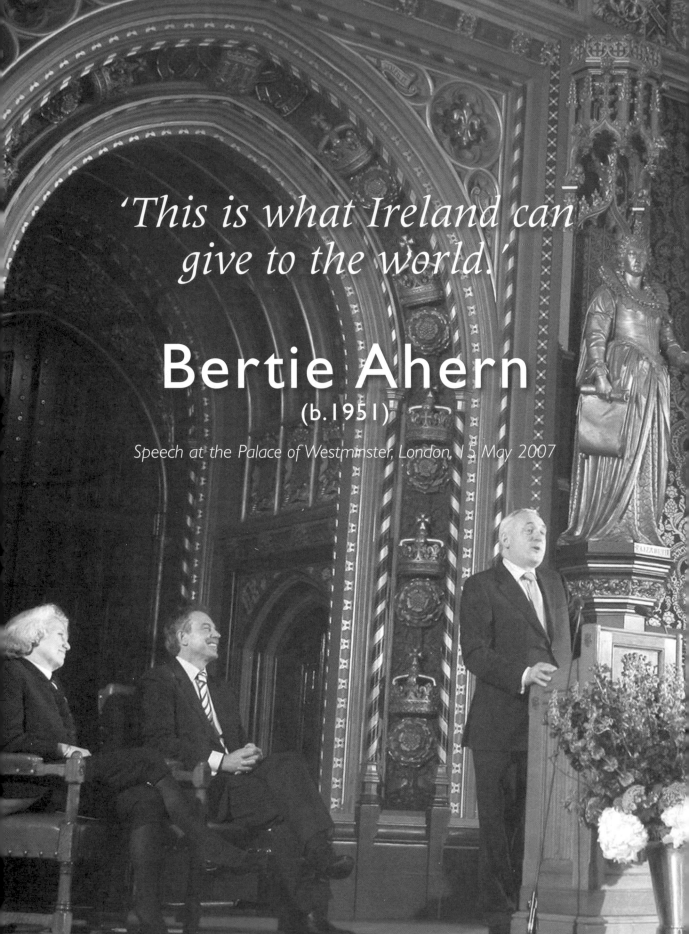

'*This is what Ireland can give to the world.*'

Bertie Ahern
(b.1951)

Speech at the Palace of Westminster, London, 15 May 2007

May 2007 was the best and the worst of times for taoiseach Bertie Ahern. The start of the month found him in the midst of a hotly contested general election campaign. Given his record during ten years of office, he might have expected to be returned convincingly. He could point to peace in Northern Ireland, unprecedented economic growth, industrial harmony, an acclaimed EU presidency, the end of mass emigration and the development of a pluralistic and cosmopolitan society. Yet Ahern was in a fight for his political life. Opinion polls suggested that Fianna Fáil was heading for defeat. Critics were disparaging about Ahern's low-key election style. And, most damagingly of all, there were persistent media stories about his financial affairs (inevitably dubbed 'Bertiegate'). On 6 May, the tánaiste Michael McDowell threatened to pull the Progressive Democrats out of the government coalition unless the taoiseach issued 'a comprehensive statement' about his personal finances. Pundits confidently predicted the end of the Ahern era. 'Fianna Fáil may be in danger of becoming the "party that will bake and eat itself",' wrote a *Village* magazine blogger, 'having overseen prosperity and renewed promise it now stands on the verge of imploding.'

This was the highly charged context in which Bertie Ahern went to the Palace of Westminster on 15 May to address a joint session of Parliament. It would be an extraordinary day of high statesmanship and door-to-door election politics. Ahern was the first Irish taoiseach to address the Houses of Parliament. It was among the highest marks of esteem that the British government could bestow – one given to just 31 world leaders since 1939, including Charles de Gaulle, Nelson Mandela, Ronald Reagan, Mikhail Gorbachev and Bill Clinton. Tony Blair, who came to power in the same year as Ahern and with whom he enjoyed a close relationship, pulled out all the stops in presenting him. 'It is a great pleasure for me to introduce a personal friend,' said Blair, 'a true friend of the British people, a man who is changing the history of his own country and of these islands, a great Irishman, An Taoiseach, Bertie Ahern.'

Ahern's own speech was beautifully crafted and skilfully delivered. 'Ireland's hour has come,' he concluded, quoting from the speech by JFK to the Oireachtas, 'a time of peace, of prosperity, of old values and new beginnings. This is the great lesson and the great gift of Irish history. This is what Ireland can give to the world.' The speech won universal praise, summed up by Miriam Lord in the *Irish Times:* 'Thanks Bertie, you did us proud.' The event had begun at midday. By the evening Ahern was back in his Dublin-Central constituency canvassing on the Navan Road.

Following the general election on 24 May 2007, Bertie Ahern was voted taoiseach by the 30th Dáil. He stands alongside Éamon de Valera as the most successful political leader in the history of the state.

Mr Speaker, Lord Speaker, Prime Minister, Distinguished Guests...

Our relationship is a partnership of people first and foremost. No two nations and no two peoples have closer ties of history and geography and of family and friendship.

Emigration was for too long a recurring theme of the Irish saga, from the horrors of the Great Famine, to dark economic times in the 20th century. Many Irish people came to this country as emigrants. And today there are hundreds of thousands of Irish-born people living in Britain today. Theirs were stories of dislocation, and stories of aspiration, and then of new lives built, new families created, new strands woven into the fabric of both our national identities. Today, there are over a hundred members of this Parliament with an Irish background. And there are millions more like them in Britain, who have gone on to new levels of success with each new generation. And, of course, the tide was not all one way. There are over 100,000 British citizens in Ireland now, a most welcome part of an ever more diverse population.

'No two nations and no two peoples have closer ties of history.'

British settlement, organized and otherwise, has given the island of Ireland a British tradition too – not just in history and language, borders and politics, but in a thriving community of unionist people proud of who they are, where they come from and what they hope for. They are a living bridge between us. The Irish government fully respects their rights and identity. We value their voice, their vision and their future contribution to the life of the island of Ireland in whatever way it should develop ...

When Prime Minister Blair and I started out together ten years ago, we were able to build on the courageous early steps that were taken by our predecessors. But the contribution of Prime Minister Blair has been exceptional. This was not a task he had to take on and not one that promised quick or easy rewards. He took it on simply because there was a chance that a great good could be achieved. Tony Blair has been a true friend to me and a true friend to Ireland. He has an honoured place in Irish hearts and in Irish history ...

'Tuesday 8 May in Belfast was a day when we witnessed events that will truly define our time and the next.'

There are certain days which define an era. More rarely there are days that define the next, that embody the turn of the tide. Too many Irish days have done so through tragedy and violence. Tuesday 8 May in Belfast was a day when we witnessed events that will truly define our time and the next. Shared devolved government, commanding support from both communities and all the parties in Northern Ireland, is now in place. Now at last the full genius and full potential of the Good Friday Agreement will unfold in the interests of all the peoples of these islands. Yes, there will be challenges ahead. But these challenges can now be faced in a climate of peace and from a foundation of partnership. There are real issues on which the people of Northern Ireland disagree. Some are the sort that face every government, and it is now the business of their politicians to find solutions based on practicality and compromise. Others are more fundamental issues of political and cultural identity.

'In these days of hope and promise we know the deep hurt and pain that linger in the hearts of so many.'

But we are now in an era of agreement – of new politics and new realities.

The world has seen Ireland's economic achievements. There is no reason why a peaceful and stable Northern Ireland should not achieve similar success. We are ready to be a partner and friend on the path to economic growth. Both parts of the island of Ireland will gain and grow ... Now let us move forward with strong practical support and increasing political confidence. The tide of history can both ebb and flow and with it our hopes and dreams. But last week's events are powerful evidence that we are moving with the tide of lasting change. There is now real strength in the consensus on the way forward. We know the unique and delicate balance that binds this process together and we are committed to doing everything in our power to protect what has been achieved.

'We are now in an era of agreement.'

Mr Speaker, Lord Speaker, in our impatience to build a better future we must remember those who have died and remember those who mourn. The conflict has left over 3700 dead and thousands more seriously injured during our lifetimes. This appalling loss has left deep scars which cannot easily be healed. I know that these are not empty words to Members of this Parliament, who have also experienced tragedy and personal loss at first hand. I remember those killed and maimed at Brighton and I remember Airey Neave MP, who was murdered so close to where we are today. There is a gnawing hunger for the truth about the loss of loved ones. The conflict has left many unanswered questions in its wake. Some of these are the subjects of ongoing or promised inquiries. In these days of hope and promise we know the deep hurt and pain that linger in the hearts of so many and for whom the journey of healing and reconciliation will never be easy.

Mr Speaker, Lord Speaker … we can all contribute to peace, in ways that are great or small, in acts of co-operation and respect, of dialogue and of resolve. This is a test for all of us. I call to mind the words of another great Irishman, Edmund Burke, who served in this Parliament, 'Nobody made a greater mistake than he who did nothing because he could do only a little.' So now we look back at history not to justify but to learn, and we look forward to the future in terms not of struggle and victories to be won, but of enduring peace and progress to be achieved together.

In that spirit, I close by recalling the words of John Fitzgerald Kennedy, the first American president to speak to the Dáil. He was an Irish-American who had deep connections of feeling and experience with Britain as well. On that day in Dublin, President Kennedy called Ireland 'an isle of destiny' and said that, 'when our hour has come we will have something to give the world'.

'Ireland's hour has come: a time of peace, of prosperity, of old values and new beginnings.'

Today, I can say to this Parliament at Westminster as John Kennedy said in Dublin, 'Ireland's hour has come.' It came, not as victory or defeat, but as a shared future for all. Solidarity has made us stronger. Reconciliation has brought us closer. Ireland's hour has come: a time of peace, of prosperity, of old values and new beginnings. This is the great lesson and the great gift of Irish history. This is what Ireland can give to the world.

Index of notable phrases

Index

For Elizabeth

Acknowledgements I wish to thank a number of friends and colleagues for their help in preparing *Great Irish Speeches*. Niamh Puirséil, before taking up her post at UCD, carried out additional research for this book. She is a fine historian in her own right (as readers of *The Irish Labour Party, 1922–73* will know) and I was lucky to be able to involve her in this project. Maurice Bric and James McGuire were extremely generous and patient when putting their expertise in Irish history at my disposal. They, along with Simon Ball and Kathryn Aldous, read early drafts. Errors that remain are of course my own, but I am profoundly grateful to all of them for the saves they have made. Liam MacMathúna kindly provided a transcript and translation of Joe Connolly's speech. Harry White was consulted on Yeats. Rory Rapple helped with classical references. Margaret O'Callaghan advised on the 19th century. Kate Breslin was indispensable. My thanks to Anthony Cheetham, who suggested writing this book. Quercus have been a pleasure to work with, not least Publishing Director, Wayne Davies, who brought his great skill and energy to the project. Rosie Anderson, aided by Sarah Chatwin, has been a sympathetic and encouraging editor. Thanks as always to Georgina Capel at Capel & Land. And special thanks to my family: my mother, Patricia, and late father (who loved parliamentary set-piece speeches), my wife, Kathryn, and our daughter, Elizabeth, to whom the book is dedicated.   *Richard Aldous*

First published in Great Britain in 2007 by

Quercus
21 Bloomsbury Square
London
WC1A 2NS

A CIP catalogue reference for this book is available from the British Library

Cloth case edition:
ISBN 978 1 84724 195 5

Book and CD Pack:
ISBN 978 1 84724 658 5

Printed in China

10 9 8 7 6 5 4 3 2 1

Picture credits
Title page & p12 Bettmann/Corbis; 15 & 19 Mary Evans Picture Library; 22 & 26 National Portrait Gallery, London; 30 Chris Hellier/Corbis; 35 TopFoto/Fotomas; 38 National Portrait Gallery, London; 41 Mary Evans Picture Library; 45 Corbis; 50 Mary Evans Picture Library; 53 National Portrait Gallery, London; 56 Bettmann/Corbis; 60 & 63 Hulton-Deutsch Collection/Corbis; 66 Corbis; 70 Hulton-Deutsch Collection/ Corbis; 75 Topical Press Agency/Getty Images; 78 Corbis; 83 Keystone/Getty Images; 87, 91 & 96 Bettmann/Corbis; 101 TopFoto; 106 Bettmann/Corbis; 110 Al Fenn/Time & Life Pictures/ Getty Images; 114 Bettmann/Corbis; 121 UPPA/TopFoto; 125 RTE Stills Library; 129 Bettmann/Corbis; 133 PA Photos; 137 Bettmann/ Corbis; 142 Bryn Colton/Corbis; 147 RTE Stills Library; 150 Pelletier Micheline/Corbis Sygma; 154 RTE Stills Library; 158 Bryn Colton/ Corbis; 163 Alan Dukes; 167 Reuters/Corbis; 171 PA Photos; 176 & 179 Nogues Alain/Corbis Sygma; 183 Cathal McNaughton/PA Photos; 188 Julian Behal/PA Photos; 192 Hadyn West/PA Photos; 195 Micah Walter/Reuters/Corbis; 199 Max Montecinos/Reuters/Corbis; 204 San Tang/PA Photos; 209 Paul Faith/PA Photos; 214 Chris Young/ PA Photos: Jacket: Walshe/Getty Images

Text credits
p177 © The Nobel Foundation 1995; p181 © The Nobel Foundation 1998

Audio credits
Éamon de Valera 'That Ireland which we dreamed of' supplied courtesy of EMI Group Archive Trust; Éamon de Valera 'The abuse of a people who have done him no wrong', Jack Lynch, Liam Cosgrave, Charles J. Haughey, Joe Connolly, John Hume, Mary Robinson, Gerry Adams, Ian Paisley and Bertie Ahern: RTÉ Libraries and Archives; Séamus Heaney: Recorded by the Swedish Radio Ltd, December 7 1995; David Trimble: Production company and broadcaster: Norwegian Broadcasting Corporation (NRK AS).

Every effort has been made to contact copyright holders. However, the publishers will be glad to rectify in future editions any inadvertent omissions brought to their attention.

Designer: Patrick Nugent
Picture researcher: Su Alexander
Project manager: Rosie Anderson
Editor: David Pickering
Proofreader: Sarah Chatwin
Indexer: Zeb Korycinska